CATHERINE TAYLOR

ILLEGITIMATELY YOURS,

MICHAEL AND ME

A memoir of secrets, adoption and DNA

Bound by the blood of the heart

—THUNDA PAIRAMA MAIROU

Illegitimately yours, Michael and Me:
A memoir of secrets, adoption and DNA

Cover designed by Leah, Shaz and Catherine

First Printing August 2019

Catherine Taylor
Visit my website at catherinetaylor.co.nz

Note from the author

This story has been constructed from memories, anecdotes and genealogical research. It is told from my memory and perspective, and other family members may have differing views. Where necessary I have changed names and identifying details to respect the privacy of people involved.
The aim of this memoir is to put the past to rest and present an account of our family history, told as honestly as possible and without malice to anyone. It's simply my story, told in my own words

TABLE OF CONTENTS

About the author

Call me Storm. Why? Because it's my real first name, but I publish under my second and maiden names, Catherine Taylor. Since 2012, I've published seven erotic romance thrillers. This is my first nonfiction, non-erotic story in which I share a deeply personal account of my life. If you're daring enough, you can find the sexy stories on my website

https://catherinetaylor.co.nz/

Part One

THE EARLY YEARS

CHAPTER ONE

CHRISTMAS 1968

Before sunrise I awoke to the stifling dry heat of an Adelaide summer. The night before had left me tired and grumpy, having stayed awake to well after midnight. At five years old I loved a good night's sleep, but not at the cost of missing out on some fun with my nine-year old brother, Michael.

At that time of year, and all through the school holidays, the heat was intense. The only way to keep cool at night was by sharing a mattress on the floor, stationed at the open front door of our house. If we were lucky, we would feel the soft breath of a cool breeze through the screen door.

We whispered and giggled, while constantly shushing each other. Our parents' bedroom was right next to the front door, and too much talking risked our being sent back to our hot, stuffy bedrooms. We could always judge by Dad's snoring when it was safe to get louder.

Our summer bed offered so much more than relief from the heat. Long after the lights had gone out we would await our nightly adventures, beginning with the activity in the two-storey bank building next door. Lights would appear in the windows as the cleaners arrived. Soon after, the music of their radio would reach our hearing.

We listened, hoping to hear our favourite songs - *Light My Fire* by The Doors or *Hey Jude* by the Beatles. Often the music would send me off to sleep, but Michael would always wake me to greet our nightly visitor.

Their arrival would begin with the echoing clop of hooves on the empty road. We would hear the squeak of our front gate, the crunch of boots on the gravel and the clinking of bottles. Soon a beam of light would dance about on the verandah.

We'd stay silent, watching a shadowy figure collect two empty milk bottles and replace them with full ones. About then, we would announce our presence with a simple greeting. The reactions of our various milkmen provided great entertainment, ranging from a panicked gasp to a string of angry muttered expletives. To their credit, none of them ever dropped a bottle, and some of the regulars got used to us and cheerfully greeted us back.

Sometimes it was us who got the fright, awoken by Dad yelling and screaming out in his sleep. We'd giggle and listen to Mum trying to soothe him.

"Wally, wake up, love, you're dreaming again. You'll wake the kids. Quieten down or I'll have to shut the windows."

Soon after, Dad would come shuffling out of the bedroom and head to the kitchen. Michael and I would follow him, knowing he would make us a cup of tea and a slice of toast. He seemed to like our company but wouldn't say much, preferring to concentrate on whatever book he was reading. He would frown and grunt off any attempt to question him about his scary dreams.

Summer nights, school holidays and lazy days filled with adventures. We both had creative imaginations which could turn the simplest things into games. Just riding our bikes around the backyard would become an epic journey. A piece of driftwood brought home from the beach became a galleon with masts of handkerchiefs on a stormy sea of grass. The skull of a dead bird, some sea shells and a few colourful stones were the prize exhibits in our museum.

Michael loved drawing and he was incredibly talented, but he also had an uncanny ability to make up exciting stories, some of which we tried to turn

4

into books. I also loved poetry and composed poems which Michael illustrated. It often turned comical when we went through every silly rhyming word to fit.

One of our favourite games was building structures with the hundreds of empty matchboxes which our old neighbour, Mr. Brook, had collected for us. Our fun was ruined when our tom cat, Big Huck, decided to spray all over them. The smell took days to dissipate from the house. It probably prompted my parents' decision to buy Michael a box of Lego that year for Christmas.

That particular grumpy morning the mattress was devoid of my brother and I was immediately curious of his whereabouts. It was rare for Michael to be out of bed before me since he stayed awake far longer than I ever did. It took a moment to realise there was something different about our previous night. We'd volunteered to go to bed early so we could wake up for some exciting event.

Wiping the sleep from my eyes, it slowly dawned on me what day it was. The previous day, Christmas Eve, we'd plotted to get a glimpse of Father Christmas, or at least hear the jingle of sleigh bells. Michael was always clever at staying awake and had promised to help me do likewise. I strained to remember the night and could only conclude he had failed.

In prior weeks, Michael had explained what Christmas would mean for us: a visit to the Magic Cave in the city to see Father Christmas, the fun of making gifts for our parents and decorations for the house, and on Christmas Day there would be new toys and coloured popcorn and all our favourite desserts. It was almost a betrayal that he hadn't woken me immediately to enjoy it with him. I launched out of bed to find him and tell him off.

Our house seemed so big back then. The front door and our makeshift bed were in the shorter section of an L-shaped hallway. The longest part was a dark world, void of windows and divided halfway by an arch and two red velvet curtains. It led all the way to the kitchen with two doors along the way, one for Michael's bedroom and the other for the living room.

Heading to the kitchen, I heard voices and laughter coming from the bedroom. Upon opening his door, I found Michael sitting on the floor with our much older brother Robin who was visiting. They were racing cars around a figure-eight racetrack. Wrapping paper was strewn about, and nearby was a giant box of Lego. It was difficult to stay cross with so much distraction, but I had serious issues to deal with.

"You didn't wake me," I pouted. "I missed seeing Father Christmas."

"Go away, we're playing."

"I want to play too."

"You can't. There are only two cars."

I stamped my foot. "I want to play and you didn't wake me to see Father Christmas."

Michael sighed impatiently and put his controller down. "I didn't see him either, but come with me and I'll show you something."

I followed him back to the front door and we went out onto the verandah where he pointed to two long, deep tracks in our gravel.

"That's how close he was to us," Michael explained. "Those tracks were made by his sleigh."

I gasped in awe and finally accepted that Father Christmas was far too clever for us. "I want to race cars."

"No, me and Robin are playing."

"I want to play too."

We returned to the bedroom with me nagging Michael all the way. He was rescued by my small scrawny body being scooped up in the arms of Robin.

"What's all this pouting and fussing?" he boomed with laughter as jolly as any Father Christmas.

I giggled, thrilled to have the attention of this tall handsome brother who smelled of Old Spice cologne. He was balding like Dad and had Mum's dark eyes. We saw him only at this time of the year when he got leave from the Navy and was able to make the 1,200 km drive from Canberra to be with us. A plane would have been much faster but Robin had a lifelong dislike of flying.

Michael and I loved his visits. It was enormous fun having our grown-up brother staying in our house, who constantly bought us gifts and took us to the movies and long drives in his car. Mum and Dad didn't own a car so it was awesome to be in something other than a bus or tram.

His visits were especially wonderful for Mum. With Robin in our home, she was jubilant and seemed at least ten years younger. Even Dad's youth was revived, with the two men looking more like best friends than father and son. Sometimes they would sneak off to the pub together and both get a good telling-off from Mum when they got home. We could tell she was never really cross with them, because she'd have a grin on her face. The only downside was all the extra drinking which went on.

Robin, Mum and Michael shared similar features, with all of them having black hair, big, dark brown eyes and olive skin. Michael's skin was even darker than theirs and starkly contrasted to my pale complexion, especially in summer. Dad and I were more alike with our bright blue eyes.

Michael and I often competed for our big brother's attention, but there was little need. Robin was generous to both of us with his time, gifts and the fun he provided.

Robin sat me up on his shoulders. "Let's go see what Father Christmas brought you."

We found Mum and Dad in the kitchen, busily preparing our Christmas lunch. There were all sorts of wonderful aromas filling the room and delicacies were spread across the Formica table. Seasoned chickens were sitting in a pan with their drumsticks tied and ready to go into the oven. A pudding was boiling away on our gas stove and orange, red and green jellies were setting in white bowls. The day promised so much excitement.

During the previous week, Mum had got out all of her special crockery which was only used at Christmas, along with my favourite tablecloth. It was silky and had scenes of an English countryside, with hunters in smart red coats astride their horses, and dogs running about between their legs.

Our entrance brought a halt to the activity but Mum and Dad were delighted to see me.

"Merry Christmas, sweetheart. Let's get your breakfast and then we'll go see what Father Christmas brought you."

"No," I pouted. "I don't want breakfast. I want to see my presents."

Of course, there was no attempt to argue with me. I usually got my way and soon we were gathered in our living room. Joining us was our old Australian terrier, Susie, who was content to distance herself and watch the proceedings from Dad's armchair.

Also watching us from the mantelpiece was our budgie, Silky. The moment Mum entered he flew across the room to perch on her shoulder and chant "pretty boy." As much as Michael and I enticed him, Silky rarely came near us. He stayed high up out of our reach, cocking his head and eyeing us suspiciously. If we could sit still and watch, he would perch on Mum's glass of port and have a drink. That morning I was more interested in a pile of brightly wrapped presents.

A twelve-inch Christmas tree sat in the window of the wall which divided living room from kitchen. A little tinsel had been wrapped around its white-tipped greenery but that was as far as any commercial decoration went. Next to it was a multitude of Christmas cards and the golden Buddha, which Dad had brought back from Japan after the War. A cotton wool beard had been added to his smiling face and a little red Santa hat to his bald head. This amusing, but rather blasphemous habit, was Dad's contribution to Christmas. Buddha didn't seem to mind and kept smiling gleefully.

I was soon tearing away at the paper. The first gift was a little disappointing, revealing a small orange woollen blanket which Mum had been knitting in the few months prior to Christmas. A pink satin bow had been added to it.

"What's this for?" I asked, somewhat disappointed.

"You'll see," Mum smiled.

The next present was way better. My determination to be a mother at five years of age was finally rewarded with a lifelike baby doll, who I instantly christened Princess. I was ready to go off and play with her, but the adults were prompting me to see if Father Christmas had brought me anything else. I feigned polite excitement upon discovering some toy jewellery and new books, which really did interest me, but nothing impressed me more than Princess.

Michael finally had to come forward to point out the obvious big lump covered up by a sheet. He helped me remove it until I was gasping and screaming with excitement. Before me was a red and white wicker pram with real tyres on the wheels and a chrome handle at one end. The blanket Mum had knitted fitted into it perfectly.

It was a truly joyful, Christmas morning. After the wrapping paper had been cleared away, the adults adjourned to the kitchen to continue preparations for Christmas lunch and imbibe their first festive drinks.

Michael went off to his bedroom to build a town with his Lego. I eventually got bored with pushing Princess around in the pram and whined until Michael allowed me to assist him with the construction of a Lego city.

If I could travel back in time, I would revisit that happy morning when I knew nothing of our family history. I would stop the clock from ticking over to the afternoon where my joy would be swallowed up with every mouthful of liquor. I would lock the door to stop the intrusion of visitors who would dispel every notion I'd ever had of my perfectly normal family.

Michael in our backyard with the bank building next door

CHAPTER TWO

GRANDMA'S HOUSE

The doorbell rang, announcing the arrival of my grandmother, aunt and cousin. Christmas was the only time of the year they made the half-hour walk to our place. Normally, it was up to us to do the visiting.

Every Sunday morning Dad, Michael and I would make the pilgrimage to Grandma's house bringing a pot of chicken broth, our garden vegetables and a variety of Mum's weekly baking. I enjoyed the walk more than the visit.

There was a ritual we observed along the way. We'd stop to admire the monkey puzzle tree which grew near the Catholic Church, then continue to the house with the white, iron diamond-patterned fence. The Samoyed which lived there would hear us coming and poke his shiny, black nose through one of the diamonds. We would then reach through and pat his fluffy, white body.

Further on we entered the shadows of several ancient Moreton Bay fig trees. Their roots were so big they had lifted the pavement and twisted up the fence. The air was thick with the smell of decaying figs, and the monstrous branches and thick foliage blocked out the sun. Dad would stop to light a cigarette, happy to wait while Michael and I played among roots which were taller than me. There was no place like it for imagining ourselves in a deep, dark jungle.

There was never any hurry to get to Grandma's house. Along the way I would pick flowers which protruded beyond the fences, gathering them into a bouquet to give to Aunty Margaret. Dad would narrate tidbits of the local history along the way. We knew the house where his own grandparents had lived and another house near Grandma's where Mum used to live before they were married.

And then we would arrive at Grandma's House. I was often struck with a sense of foreboding as I got my first glimpse. Nestled between other similar style houses, Grandma's looked like a classic haunted house.

It was badly neglected. The central wooden door was scratched and splintered and still had a few patches of dark brown paint. Weeds grew tall along the front and covered most of the path leading to the steps of the bullnose-roofed verandah. On either side of the door ripped, tattered curtains were tightly closed across two filthy front windows.

Dad would mutter under his breath before giving us his usual warning, "Watch where you walk, don't eat anything, even if Aunty Margaret offers you something, and don't step in the cat shit."

We knew the drill and always took our last gulp of fresh air as we waited to be let in. When the door opened we were hit by the thick, stale smell of cat shit and urine. Years of Sunday visits had given us a tolerance to the smell and we were experts at navigating any recent deposits left by the cats. The floorboards of the hallway were layered in a thick film of cat waste and filth. The wallpaper was faded and scratched to shreds, with just a glimpse of the pattern it once had. The few old family portraits which hung about were obscured by caked dust.

Greeting us, Aunty Margaret's smiling face was much more welcoming. She was always pleased to see us and oblivious to the state of the house. If Dad grumbled about the mess, she would snap back at him and tell him to mind his own business. Mostly, he ignored it and seemed genuinely happy to see his youngest sister.

The hallway led to the dark living room where the culprits of the filth were stationed like sentinels on every piece of furniture. A multitude of cats would watch our intrusion into their domain, the older ones sitting statue-still with stern observation while the younger ones roamed about. Kittens popped up everywhere and played about on the table and floor.

In a bed under the window Grandma was propped up with pillows, holding a glass of beer or stout, while dropping the ash of her cigarette onto the counterpane. Her tabby, Little Man, rested up against her with his smug expression at his pride of place.

There was little room to move about with the massive oak dining table taking up most of the space. It was littered with dirty dishes, books, newspapers and cats. There were a few wooden and leather chairs which had to be checked for poop before sitting down. Two leadlight cabinets lined one wall and seemed to be the most popular post for cats, where they could be high up and observe every move we made.

Michael and I would reluctantly head to the bed to greet Grandma. She was a tiny woman with grey hair pulled back in a bun, a toothless mouth,

11

washed out blue eyes and a face as wrinkled as a prune. She would barely respond to our greeting and always seemed sour. Through the years I knew her, there was never any grandmotherly affection for Michael and me.

The only person who received kindness from her was our cousin, Susan. She was Aunty Margaret's daughter and in the middle age range between Michael and me, which made me last in the pecking order.

I always struggled to understand why my brother would change so abruptly whenever she was around. Susan was rarely nice to me and took great delight in teaming up with Michael to make me the object of their torment. They would whisper and laugh while looking at me. She would tell me they had secrets which I wasn't allowed to know, or they would go into her bedroom and shut me out, not that I particularly wanted to be in there.

The bedroom came off the living room and wasn't much different from the rest of the house. It reeked of urine from buckets still unemptied. All the furniture was old and scratched, and the bedlinen was dirty and crushed under piles of old clothes, books and boxes. The other two bedrooms were strictly off limits, but a few daring explorations had revealed them to be just as crammed with rubbish and broken furniture.

I rarely saw the kitchen, and the few times I did it wasn't pleasant. It was hoarded with piles of newspapers and filthy dishes and blackened pots. There were even buckets containing human waste kept by the back door. Cockroaches roamed about on every surface. The smell was horrific.

Throughout our visits my bladder was trained to hold on until I could get home. The toilet was barely usable, being a broken brick outhouse in the backyard with no door and surrounded by a jungle of tall weeds. Sometimes Michael and Susan went out the back to play, but I was content to leave them to it.

It was safer to stay in the living room with the adults. Dad would take his place at the table to chat with Aunty Margaret, barely acknowledging Grandma. A glass of port would be put in front of him, cigarettes would be lit and the animated chatter would begin. It was usually about their latest wins on the horses. I learned a lot about horseracing from those conversations.

There are several incidents within Grandma's house which remain firmly rooted in my memory. The first was a time when I was about twelve years of age and had reluctantly agreed to stay over with my cousin. It was the longest night of my life. While my cousin slept, I sat on the end of the bed in dim light, choking on stale, acidy air and very conscious of scuttling noises in the room. At some time during the night, I went out to the main room which still had the light on.

Most of the cats were awake, the kittens playing on the floor while the old cats seemed to be permanently fixed in their positions. Grandma's bed had been further invaded by my cousin's two dogs, a wiry-haired terrier named Kaiser and an albino kelpie named Lucky. In the quiet and amid the mews of kittens came the squeaky shrill of guinea pigs, darting across the floor to hide under the cabinets. Only the kittens showed any interest and I still marvel how all these animals seemed to coexist in harmony.

If the staring eyes of cats wasn't fearful enough that night, I was suddenly assaulted with a sight I will never forget, the stuff which horror movies have never captured quite the same for me. My intrusion into that room caused the scatter of the only creatures bothered by my presence - the cockroaches in their hundreds, blooming outwards to the edges of the table, down the legs and across the floor, evoking the crazed attention of kittens which leaped among them.

I rapidly retreated into the bedroom and sat shaking and tightly cross-legged on the end of the bed, praying for the oncoming of morning. I grabbed the closest book, a photographic picture book entitled *Walkabout* by Donald Gordon Payne. Eventually I managed to lose myself in it and forget the horror beyond the door. I never stayed in that house again.

Another bizarre occurrence was during a visit shortly after Grandma had bought a horse for my cousin, a teenager by then, who'd had horse-riding lessons since childhood. On a drunken autumn day, Aunty Margaret decided this horse was being neglected with my cousin having recently started a secretarial course and immersing herself in a social life.

Going to the nearby parklands where the horse was stabled, Aunty Margaret led the horse all the way back to the house. Dad's mutterings became quite audible when we walked in to see this creature standing impassively in the main room with the rest of the menagerie.

"What? It's not enough this place is crawling with cats and every other vermin," Dad commented with calm disapproval. "Now you're going to keep a bloody horse here too."

"It's going to be raining all week," Aunty Margaret chided him back. "I'm not walking all that way to the park in the rain to feed this thing while Susan isn't here. It can stay here the week."

Grandma told him to shut up and mind his own business. Dad grumbled some more and then took his usual place at the table with his glass of port and no one seemed bothered by the elephant, or rather horse, in the room.

The memories I have of this house are bizarre and have raised many questions throughout my lifetime. How was it that my cousin was forced to live in these conditions without intervention from authorities? How had Grandma and Aunty Margaret allowed it to get to this state? Why had nothing been done about a home in such obvious shambles?

In my most recent return to Adelaide in April 2019, I visited the house and wondered if the people living in it knew anything of its morbid history. Over the years I'd made a few of my own discoveries, especially after meeting up with my ninety-year-old second cousin Ken who, like me, was doing our family history.

The house was first purchased in 1927 by my grandfather and was the home Dad and his three sisters, Elsie, Iris and Margaret, were raised in. Granddad passed away in 1947 from bowel cancer and Grandma was left inconsolable, such was the love affair she shared with him.

Ken told me of having walked in on them one afternoon and catching them in a freestanding bath together in the kitchen, splashing each other and laughing like children. They were unperturbed by his interruption and only shocked him further as they leant in towards each other to share a sultry kiss. Ken, who was just a boy at the time, made a hasty retreat.

Back then the house was bright, cheerful, clean and tidy. Ken remembered Grandma as a feisty, cheerful soul who often spoke in Finnish and the house was lively with the constant visits of relatives. Granddad was a fireman and a much loved brother among his eight siblings, but Grandma was his light and love, as he was to her.

During the forties Dad, their only son, had gone away to war then volunteered to help out in the occupation of Japan. During that time, he was summoned home with the news his father was dying. He had passed away before Dad got back.

It seemed death had taken two souls away that day. Grandma grieved deeply for her husband. She became lifeless, angry and bitter towards everyone. Aunties Elsie and Iris were living in Victoria and Aunty Margaret was recently married. Dad spent as little time at home as he could, spending most of his hours at the pub down the road where he worked. The house had begun a decline which continued until its fateful day thirty years later.

When I was fourteen and away on camp, I returned to learn the house had burned down, taking out many cats and all the guinea pigs. Aunty Margaret made the front page of the paper for rescuing Grandma after a kerosene heater apparently went up in flames. With no insurance, the local church bought the house for a meagre sum in 1977. It was restored and now has a seven-figure value.

I was always happy to return home where everything was clean and tidy; where our four cats lived outside and Michael would be nice to me again. I often felt sorry for Susan for having to live in such conditions. What I didn't understand then was how close I came to suffering the same fate.

Christmas 1968 was when it first occurred to me, and I remember how much the thought frightened me. I had nightmares of being made to live there with the filth, the cats and Grandma.

My understanding of the frailty of human beings began with that house, and to this day and through many years of social work, I've never seen worse conditions. To me, it was a habitat of despair and bitterness. They had lost faith in life and their hope for happiness had been abandoned.

I've known those feelings. I've written about them in poetry when depression has gripped me and when agoraphobia has held me prisoner. I'm sad for what they suffered. It was Aunty Margaret who gave me a chance to have a completely differently life and I'll always be deeply grateful to her.

CHAPTER THREE

REVELATIONS

Even at the age of five, I had an ominous foreboding about that Christmas and the once-a-year visit from Grandma, Aunty Margaret and Susan. It was as if I suspected their presence in our home as being unpleasant. Maybe it was the certainty of adults getting drunk, and Michael and Susan tormenting and excluding me.

They seemed to bring the surly mood of Grandma's house with them, along with the smell of cats, tobacco and alcohol. Susan wasted no time in getting Michael alone and having me removed from his bedroom. Telling on them only made things worse, with their singsong taunts of me being a tattletale.

That year my baby doll, Princess, paid the price with Susan and Michael throwing her across the room to each other, keeping her out of my reach. Finally when I tattled again, we were made to stay in the living room and play. They sat on Dad's armchair together where they could pretend to look at a picture book, while giggling and whispering about me.

By then my attention was far more focused on what was happening in the kitchen where the adults were drinking. I could hear my happy Christmas being swallowed up with every glass of port, beer and whisky. Laughter was slowly evolving into raised voices and unchecked profanity. Even Grandma was talking but had nothing nice to say.

I sat curled up in a chair watching television, trying to lose myself in a black and white movie about Christmas and ignore how miserable and alone I felt. Michael and Susan were too busy playing and enjoying my isolation to take much notice of what was going on, but I listened to everything, including my name being mentioned several times.

Dad and Robin were trying to tell everyone to calm down but the women were soon drowning them out.

"It's all your fault," Grandma screeched. "Wally had no business getting tangled up with the likes of you. You're nothing but the black bitch from Birkenhead."

16

Mum's furious response came with a string of swear words which would make a sailor blush. Sober, Mum was quiet, gentle and ladylike. After a half a flagon of port, she was volatile and not one to back down against anyone. I never saw an affectionate moment between Mum and Grandma.

It wasn't the first time I'd heard Grandma's 'black bitch from Birkenhead' comment. In later years it was something Mum and I laughed about, but on that day it was the trigger which sent my world into chaos.

As the yelling got louder, Michael and Susan got quieter and we were finally united in our misery over the drunken arguments in the kitchen. Michael even invited me to join him and Susan on the armchair, but I was too withdrawn and frightened to move.

Inevitably, the violence caught up with us when Aunty Margaret came into the living room, muttering and angry. The first thing she saw was Michael and Susan sitting on the armchair together and her fury went up a notch.

"What do you think you're doing?" she screamed at them. "You get away from my daughter."

Susan was dragged to her feet while Michael shrank back in the chair. Aunty Margaret hovered over him, clutching Susan's arm.

"You're no good. You're a horrible boy. You stay away from my daughter."

Her attention turned to me and for a long time her eyes burrowed into mine. "You don't belong here either. You're my daughter. I'm taking you home with me."

I was terrified and had no idea what she was talking about. All I could picture was being made to live in that horrible house with people I didn't particularly like.

She took my hand and I started screaming and bawling as she pulled me to my feet and began to drag me out of the room. I looked at Michael and he whispered his intention to get Mum. Susan was bawling too and begging her to stop, but we were nearly to the front door before rescue came.

Up until then the fights had always been verbal, but that day it went up a notch. Mum came flying up and grabbed Aunty Margaret by the hair before she could walk out the door. I slipped away from her and Michael grabbed me back against himself as the two women became vicious, slapping at each other's faces.

Dad and Robin finally appeared and got the women separated but the verbal exchanges continued.

"She's my daughter," Aunty Margaret insisted. "You tell her or I will. She's not staying here. She's coming home with me."

Dad got furious then, and told her to shut her mouth, but Aunty Margaret looked at me and continued. "They didn't tell you. She's not your mother. I'm your mother. They're not your family."

By then Grandma had joined us, but her drunken fury was addressed solely at Robin. "You're just as bad as your black bitch of a mother. This is as much your fault and you think you can just forget about it."

Robin sneered and laughed bitterly before gathering me up in his arms. He left them to it, taking me and Michael back to Michael's bedroom where I cried until I couldn't breathe. Robin and Michael tried everything to comfort me but I was terrified. All I could think about was being taken away from Mum and Dad and made to live in Grandma's house.

I eventually fell asleep. When I awoke later that night, Mum wrapped me in her arms and I finally felt safe again. Peace had been restored and the house was quiet again. The smell of port was still strong on Mum's breath but I didn't care. She knew what I wanted to know, what I desperately needed to hear.

"You're our daughter and nobody will ever take you away from us."

There was a fierce conviction to her words which made me feel secure. She took me down to the lounge and Dad came in from the kitchen. He frowned at me.

"Are you alright, girl?"

"Yes, Dad."

"There's a good movie about to start. You want to watch it?"

I nodded cheerfully.

Dad took his usual spot on the floor, lying on his belly in front of the television. I sat astride his back, grinning at the shiny bald patch on his head and sniffing the scent of 'Californian Poppy' hair oil. Mum sat in her chair and brought out her darning or whatever knitting project she was working on.

I was happy again, sitting in my favourite spot and watching a movie. It was my job alone to strike the match lighting each of Dad's cigarettes, a task I usually had to share with Michael, but not that night. My brothers left us to it and went back to the bedroom to race cars.

Nothing was said about the absence of our visitors or Aunty Margaret trying to take me home with her. I didn't want to talk about it and Mum and Dad wanted even less to bring it up.

But I never forgot that Christmas or the words spoken. Like many other things heard in drunken conversations, it was filed away in my mind. From an early age I knew my family had something odd about it, but not knowing meant nothing would change, or so I believed.

CHAPTER FOUR

1969

The Sunday visits to Grandma's house had stopped, and for a while Michael and I went to Sunday school at the Salvation Army. We weren't regular attendees but I liked being there. The Bible stories captured my attention and we got to make things and sing songs. The idea of an all-powerful being watching over us appealed to me.

Later in my twenties, when I reconnected with a much deeper faith in God, it was in the Salvation Army I found fellowship. It was through their actions of demonstrating acceptance of people, regardless of sin and circumstance, which helped shape my understanding of God.

It was also through attending Sunday school that my passion for theatre was kindled. At four years of age, I landed the title role of Susie Snowflake in a Sunday school production to be held at the Adelaide Town Hall. Before a huge audience, I confidently strutted the stage in a sparkly leotard and white cotton balls, singing my heart out. The applause was exhilarating and all I wanted after that was to be star of stage or screen. I never quite achieved my objective but did clock up nearly forty years of acting in theatre and film.

I have fond memories of the Salvation Army, the friendly people in their smart uniforms and the music of the brass band, but I especially liked the way they treated us. I sensed no disapproval of Mum and Dad whenever they showed up to a Sunday night meeting after an afternoon on the booze. They were still warmly welcomed as if everything was normal. It was an immense source of embarrassment to be out in public with my drunken parents.

It happened frequently and caused me constant anxiety, forever fearful they would do something which would draw attention to us. I often declined outings if I thought Mum and Dad would be drinking. There were school productions I missed out on for fear they would show up drunk. It was better to be home where their inebriation didn't bother me so much, where I could lose myself in a book or a movie.

By the age of seven, I had dealt with several drunken incidents which had mortified me and even exposed me to the possibility of intervention by authorities. One of them was after a Sunday visit to Grandma's when my very drunken Dad stumbled and fell down outside the Catholic Church. A substantial crowd was gathered, preparing to go in for evening mass, and those standing nearby came to help him. They quickly backed off when they smelled the booze and saw the state he was in. I became the focus of their attention with someone suggesting the police be called. Giving Dad a swift kick, I begged him to get up. The mention of police got him to his feet, but some of the people didn't want me to go with him.

I had to get surly and yell back at them. "He's alright. He just fell and we're going home now, so leave us alone."

Another time, I had spent the day at the pub where Dad worked, which was right in the middle of the city. He'd only worked half the day, but had stayed on to drink with friends, one of whom had given him a crayfish. On our homeward walk down Rundle Mall we stopped at another pub and he drank some more. It was getting dark when we finally headed to the bus stop, but then Dad decided he was hungry and wanted a bit of that crayfish.

I groaned and sat down with him on a seat, watching him breaking open the spindly legs to get to the white meat inside. Some of the meat fell on the pavement and Dad looked like he would topple over when he bent down to pick it up. Of course, his swaying and rather vulgar display of eating the crayfish drew lots of attention, including that of two police officers.

Dad saw them heading our way and scowled. "You better get yourself home without me, girl. These two bastards want a piece of me."

He pulled out some money and handed it to me. "You know where the taxis line up, jump into the first one in line and tell him where we live. Tell your mother I'll be home later."

I did as he said, feeling a little relieved to be away from Dad's antics and stirred by the excitement of walking through the city and catching a taxi on my own. When I arrived home alone, Mum was furious and refused to go to the police station the next morning to bail him out. Michael eventually ran down to Grandma's house to get Aunty Margaret to do it, but Mum was still talking about kicking Dad out. I bawled and begged her not to send Dad away until she finally relented. I rarely saw my parents argue about anything, but that week there was certainly some simmering tension in our home.

It didn't stop Mum sending me to the pubs with Dad if he planned to make a day of it. After the crayfish scandal, my presence always guaranteed he got home in a reasonable state. He praised me up several times for being so grown up and getting home safe, but it was more about expressing the relief he felt. I think he was genuinely ashamed for having neglected me.

As the sixties came to an end, I was getting used to being 'grown up' and looking after myself. I was also becoming familiar with being alone. There were weekends when Michael wasn't with us, though nobody talked about where he went, and then came the times he would simply jump on his pushbike and ride away, not to be seen for a day or two.

Dad took time off work to look for him but Michael always came back on his own. He would tap on my window during the night and wake me up to let him in. We would climb into his bed where I would cuddle him, just so relieved to have him back. In the morning, nothing was really said. Dad would be a bit grumbly and quiet, but Mum just seemed pleased to see him.

Whenever I asked Michael why he ran away, he had no definitive answer. "I don't know. I get angry and want to ride my bike and sometimes I just keep riding."

It took me years to discover the reasons behind the despair Michael was suffering and the horror he was yet to go through. Back then, in my first childhood home, everything was so normal to me; I had no reason to ask questions.

I irritably accepted that we had to make regular trips to the Adelaide Children's Hospital for Michael's leg. During the day he wore a leg iron, and at night it was changed to something which looked more like half a plaster cast with straps. All I knew was something had happened to his leg when he was little and it needed to be braced.

Michael also had an unnatural fear of having his hair cut and my parents would have to coax and bribe him with treats to get the job done. I think they would have let him grow his hair long but there was no getting around the strict school rules.

When I was six, I had my first haircut when Mum got sick. She spent a long time in bed and Dad took time off work to look after her and us. I remember this well as it was highly amusing to see Dad doing the jobs Mum usually did. Michael and I got to spend a lot of time with him and had so much fun.

Dad seemed determined to get us out the house. We would go on day-long hikes, following the tram tracks to Glenelg Beach. Our favourite destination was the playground in the parklands which had a treehouse with a slide, a sandpit and seesaws, and a creek which ran for miles. We would follow it, climbing up and down the banks and stopping to catch tadpoles to take home to observe their fascinating transformation into frogs.

At home he taught us how to make a kite and a terrarium, the latter somehow achieved with a strip of cloth, soaked in kerosene and wrapped around an empty port flagon. We read stories and watched much more television than usual. Dad did all the housework and meals, though Michael and I were often sent down to the shop to get fish and chips.

Michael didn't run away at all during those weeks and we spent hours building cities out of Lego and coming up with new adventures. He seemed to understand how sick Mum was and was worried she would leave us. It was during that time he started to talk about things I'd never known.

"I have two Mums, but I haven't seen the other one for a long time. She used to take me out places and buy me things. Sometimes there were other people with us who called her Mary and I think I have another Grandma."

I was fascinated and recalled the things Aunty Margaret had said at Christmas. Michael was the first to mention the word 'adopted' and explained that Mum and Dad had gone out one day and brought me home with them.

"We're not supposed to talk about anything."

It was then he showed me something which he kept buried in his drawer. It was a 'cradle roll' certificate from the Salvation Army. On it was printed the name 'Michael Nicholas Robinson.'

"But your name is Taylor. Michael Nicholas Taylor," I argued. "Like me and Mum and Dad."

"That's what I was called when I started school, but there was another name I've heard as well, Michael Nicholas Mairou."

Michael told me he had taken the certificate from Mum's wardrobe and there were many other papers there, some with that name on them. I suddenly wanted to see if my name was different too and felt the excitement of adventure and discovery.

23

At that time, some of my favourite stories were 'The Three Investigators' books by Alfred Hitchcock and 'The Secret Seven' by Enid Blyton. With questions needing answers, I decided we should also become investigators and solve the mysteries surrounding our lives.

When Mum eventually got better, Dad returned to work. Life returned to normal but the sense of mystery remained. During school holidays Mum would have to take us grocery shopping with her. One day we begged her to let us stay home and she gave in, after giving us a long list of instructions to follow. As soon as she was gone, we were on the case.

The excitement left me breathless as we entered Mum and Dad's bedroom. It was a beautiful room with the bed always neatly made and covered in an orange bedspread. Next to it was the red iron cot where I slept for the first four years of my life.

There was an alcove with two French doors which opened up onto the front verandah. Above the bed was a huge ornate ceiling rose in which I would see strange faces if I stared long enough, a game I liked to play whenever I climbed into bed with Mum.

Mum and Dad each had a locked cupboard for clothing. The keys were kept on top of each cupboard and Michael had to get a chair to retrieve them. We started with Mum's wardrobe, opening the doors and standing back to admire the beautiful dresses which Mum rarely wore. She had shown me them many times, telling me about the dances she attended at The Palais in Semaphore. Her face always lit up when she spoke of those times.

But we weren't there to see dresses and soon we were removing boxes and taking them to the bed to open. Michael had spoken to me a lot about how important it was to keep it secret if we found anything. It was a truly exciting and fun adventure which soon became quite serious.

With some boxes containing jewelry, I had soon relinquished the investigative work to Michael, preferring to don myself with rings, necklaces and clip-on earrings.

"I found something," Michael said, staring at a piece of paper.

My attention was back on the job as he held up my immunisation card. Instead of Storm Catherine Taylor, it read Storm Catherine Peters.

"That's Aunty Margaret's name," I frowned. "And Susan's."

It was the name they'd inherited from Aunty Margaret's short marriage to William Peters. It was also Susan's last name.

"I'm not Peters," I grumbled. "I'm Taylor."

"But Aunty Margaret said she was your mother."

Suddenly I wasn't so enthralled about our adventure. "She's not my mother."

When Michael brought out another paper and started studying it. I moved in for a closer look and could see that ominous word at the top.

"What does adoption mean?"

He finally looked at me. "It means you had different parents once, and then you were adopted. This says Mum and Dad adopted you in January 1964 just after your first birthday. I think Aunty Margaret is your mum, which means Susan is your sister."

Michael hadn't realized how much that information would upset me. When I started bawling, he could see how much trouble we'd be in if Mum found out about our snooping. He quickly put everything back exactly how he'd found it and then spent a very nerve-wracking time trying to calm me down and cheer me up before Mum got home.

"It doesn't mean anything," he told me. "Mum and Dad won't let anyone take us away from them, even if they aren't really our real Mum and Dad."

"Are you adopted too?"

"Yeah, probably."

"Does that mean you're not my brother?"

"No. I'm your brother and you're my sister and Mum and Dad are our parents."

"Is Robin adopted too?"

Michael wasn't sure about that. "I don't know. He's way older than us and his last name is Clifford. He calls Mum, 'Mum' but he calls Dad 'Wally' but he's still our brother. You can't tell anyone we know this stuff or I'll get in heaps of trouble. It's got to be our secret and nobody must know."

"What about Susan?"

"No, we can't tell her either."

It helped knowing Susan wouldn't be part of our secret, but mostly I didn't want Michael in trouble. I didn't want him to get sad again and run away. We were in this together, inspiring some fortitude to keep me from blurting out everything when Mum got home.

It also helped knowing how much we were loved by our parents. I'd seen Mum's fierce attack on Aunty Margaret thwarting her attempts to take me away, and I felt assured there was nothing to worry about. The whole business was best forgotten. In days to come, I would have much worse to worry about.

CHAPTER FIVE

1970

The seventies arrived with my 7th birthday in early January. Robin had come for Christmas then returned to Canberra, but he sent me a beautiful birthday card with a ballerina on the front. It was summer again, school holidays and lots of fun to be had with Michael.

By then, I really didn't care if Aunty Margaret was my real mother, as long as she didn't try to take me away again. It was a little weird to think of Susan being my sister, but I certainly wasn't going to tell her that. I liked knowing something she didn't. Michael and I had a secret we shared, but I had no idea he had other secrets which tormented him. As far as I knew, he was as happy as I was.

Neither of us liked our parents getting drunk every weekend, but it did provide an opportunity to get up to mischief, some of it incredibly dangerous. By 7pm on a Saturday night after an afternoon's drinking, Mum was often in bed and Dad asleep on the floor in front of the television. We were left to our own devices.

One time, we got Dad's special knife with the pointy blade and deer antler handle. Drawing some rings on our outhouse door, we practised throwing it and hitting the target. Another time, we got hold of some darts and threw them at each other. I wasn't squeamish at the sight of blood and not particularly bothered by the pain of getting stabbed. I was having too much fun to let a little pain bother me. We even got some matches and set some grass on fire.

Sometimes we cooked something with just a glimpse of a recipe. We improvised with ingredients and made some disgusting creations which were impossible to eat, though we certainly tried. Whatever mischief Michael suggested, I joined in without question. He was my big brother, my hero and my best friend.

He sometimes showed me his secret treasures, things I had no idea of where they'd come from. Odd things, like cologne and rings and even diving equipment, a snorkel and a spear gun. And then, one day, the police came to our house.

27

Michael and I sat together on the armchair while Mum and Dad stood talking in the room with these tall, foreboding men in their uniforms. While they talked, Michael whispered to me, "Hide it." He tapped me on the back and I reached behind, not taking my eyes from the adults, and let him pass me a wad of dollar bills. I pushed it up the sleeve of my jumper and ran off to my bedroom. Nobody took any notice of me, or so I thought.

When I was safely away from them, I looked at what I had taken from him and was astounded by the sight of the most money I'd ever seen in my life. I was terrified, wondering if I would go to jail, especially when I heard them talking and fossicking about in Michael's bedroom.

It was an awful experience which left me shaken and upset long after the police were gone. I heard Mum and Dad lecturing Michael and him being sent to bed. This was the one time I didn't want to be part of Michael's mischief.

I thought my part in it had gone undetected but Dad came up to my room and didn't look happy. He sat on the bed with me.

"Where's the money?"

I started bawling. "In my doll's house."

He sighed. "Michael is heading for big trouble and we can't stop him, but we've tried. It's not all his fault and I can forgive him for most of it. I can't forgive him if he gets you involved. He stole money from someone and that's wrong, and you helping him is wrong."

He retrieved the money and left, leaving me to bawl alone on my bed. Even Mum didn't come up as she normally would have done whenever I was upset. It was a harsh punishment. Nothing crushed me more than to hear the disappointment in Dad's voice.

He must have said something similar to Michael because he never involved me again, at least not intentionally. Soon after that incident, I saw Michael leave our school at lunchtime and I followed him. My heart broke a little as I watched him break into a house through the window.

I went back to school and said nothing to anyone. A couple of days later the police visited our home again and found more stolen items. Dad was summoned home from work and other people turned up at our house. Michael was crying, hysterical and begging Mum not to let them take him away.

Mum was arguing angrily with these people and even swearing at them. Dad was trying to keep the situation calm and talk rationally, but in the end Michael was taken away. I was frightened and confused by my parents' inability to stop bad people hurting our family.

Mum and Dad had to go to court to see him and we'd all expected Michael to come home. Instead the authorities in charge stood up and recommended Michael spend some time in an institution - Glandore Boys' Home - and the judge agreed. My parents had to come home and tell me Michael wouldn't be coming home for a few months.

I was inconsolable and angry at everyone, but especially at Mum and Dad for allowing them to take him. My belief that Michael and I could not be taken away from them was shattered. It incited a fear that I could no longer ignore and I demanded answers.

"I know Aunty Margaret is my mother. I know Michael has another mother too. I want to know why. Is Robin adopted too? He has a different name too. His name is Clifford."

My parents were stunned by how much I knew and it was Dad who got most upset.

"You and Michael have no other Mum and Dad but us. And that's all there is to say about it."

But I was persistent. Mum and Dad had never chided us for talking back or having an opinion, so I wasn't about to let go of it. Finally Mum gave in and reluctantly asked what I wanted to know. I wanted to know everything.

"Dad and I couldn't have our own children," she explained. "We had a little baby once, a little boy and he died, because there was something wrong with our blood. The doctors told us that we couldn't have children and we were very upset. One day, the Salvation Army asked us if we wanted a little boy and we met his mother. She was very young and on her own and wanted us to look after him while she worked, so we did. She used to visit him and take him out on holidays and weekends, but then she stopped coming around. We don't know what happened to her, but Michael was our son from the moment he came to us."

"What about me?"

"Aunty Margaret was living with Grandma because her husband was not very nice. Then she had Susan and it was very hard to live without money.

She had to work and so she said that Dad and I could have her. We were so excited and bought a cradle and toys and I knitted baby clothes, but when Susan was born, Grandma wouldn't let Aunty Margaret give her to us."

By then, Mum had drunk enough to talk freely, and though I didn't understand it all, I absorbed every detail. Dad had calmed himself down after a few ports, and decided to join in on the conversation.

"Aunty Margaret knew how much we wanted a baby so she had another one and gave her to us, and that was you. We went to court and signed papers so that it officially made you our daughter. We weren't able to do that for Michael, which is why those people wouldn't listen to us. That wouldn't ever happen to you."

It was the answer I needed to hear, and for the time being I didn't want to know anything else. My curiosity had been sated and I felt secure again, except in my concern for Michael. I wanted to understand why he did things which caused him trouble, why he stole things and ran away all the time.

Mum and Dad explained that Michael was troubled before he came to them. His mother, Mary, was young, single and had little support from anyone. There was no financial assistance available and she had no choice but to work. At some stage, he'd been put into the foster system.

He was two years old before he came to my parents. He had nightmares which drove him to hide under the bed until Mum could coax him out. She would stay with him all night or bring him into bed with her and Dad. Sometimes they awoke to find him hiding under their bed.

They had wanted to adopt him, but his mother wouldn't allow it, insisting she had every intention of having Michael back with her. When she stopped coming for visits, Mum and Dad gave their surname to him and he became Michael Nicholas Taylor.

Mum and Dad were always gentle, loving people, strongly opposed to any physical discipline of children. Even when they were drunk there was never any yelling at us or anything physically abusive. If anything, they were over-indulgent and allowed us far too much freedom. Their patience with Michael was extraordinary. They loved him as their own, and regardless of what the authorities thought he was their son as much as he was my brother.

The first permitted visit to Michael in Glandore Boys' Home was heart-wrenching. When we had to leave, Michael was crying and screaming for

Mum. She couldn't go back after that. Dad and I continued the visits and it was never as bad as that first one.

Michael seemed to have accepted his circumstances but he was very different. The spark had gone out of him, and he was oddly compliant and polite to the people who worked there. He talked about the woodwork and art he was doing. I still have some of the things he made during that time.

I wrote letters every week and drew pictures for him which I was delighted to see stuck up on the wall above his bed in the ward. Dad brought him anything he asked for, including an unassembled model of an ancient galleon which he had seen in a shop. It was expensive, intricate and meant to be tackled by someone much older, but Michael constructed it perfectly, every delicate detail.

Mum and Dad continued to fight for him and, with the help of a social worker, Michael eventually came home. I was ecstatic to have my brother back with us, but it didn't take long to see how much he had changed. He was constantly withdrawn and preferred to be in his room alone. He had no new games or adventures for us to try, preferring to draw and listen to music.

It was night times we found connection again. Michael would knock on the wall between our bedrooms to check if I was still awake, and I would knock back. This went on until we were sure our parents were asleep and then I'd go into his bedroom and hop into bed with him. We would cuddle up together and listen to the radio and the music of Alice Cooper, The Beatles and Deep Purple.

When I first tried to question Michael about Glandore, he became agitated and refused to talk about it, so I let it go. I just wanted him to be happy again, to be back to his old self. There were a few glimpses of it during those nights, when we talked and giggled the way we used to. We also got up a few times to make pancakes which always tasted horrible.

One time Michael had just made the batter when we heard Dad yelling out in his sleep, a sure signal he would soon be up out of bed. We cleaned up furiously but there was no time to get rid of the jug of batter. Michael got a chair and climbed up to hide it on top of a cupboard before we scrambled back to our own beds.

It wasn't until months later, when we were packing to move house, the jug was found. By then, the contents had dried up and fluffy black and white fungus was growing in it. Mum simply cleaned it up and didn't pursue the matter. Fifty years later, I still have that jug and cherish it, because it evokes the memory of that night.

For a few months life had returned to normal, but troubled times were brewing. Our landlord had sold our house and we had to move out. None of us wanted a change of home. Michael was also grieving the loss of his beloved tabby, Big Huck, which he had brought home as a kitten. We'd named him Huck after one of our favourite stories, *Huckleberry Finn* by Mark Twain, and 'Big' was added when he grew bigger than any cat we'd ever seen. Our pets were an important part of our lives and Michael was particularly fond of them. Losing Big Huck devastated him.

Dad found us a house in another suburb where we could still go to the same school, but it had none of the character of our first home. It was smaller and attached to another house. Everything was smaller: the street it was on, the rooms and our play areas. The front garden was just a concrete verandah and a thin strip of dirt. The backyard was a patch of lawn and gravel, half as big as our last one and lacking any trees. I could see how much Michael hated it, and he was particularly agitated the week before we were due to move.

The day before we moved in he ran away again, and this time stayed away longer than ever. Every night after work, Dad walked the city streets hoping to find him and bring him home before any trouble could ensue. Finally, Mum and Dad had no choice but to alert the authorities.

The police eventually brought him home and, soon after, the judicial system decided he needed harsher rehabilitation. They sent him to a place called Windana Remand Centre which was on the same grounds as Glandore Boys' Home but with much stricter conditions.

After his stint in Glandore, Michael had changed and lost his joy of life but within the walls of Windana, his life was changed forever.

CHAPTER SIX

1970 – 1974

My life also changed with the move to our new house. I felt lonely without Michael and spent a good deal of my time reading and watching television. I was looking forward to visiting him in Windana and imagined it would be like Glandore, with a playground and trees and grass and boys running around making lots of noise.

Instead, it was that first visit which gave me a small insight into what Michael had suffered. On arriving, I was disappointed to see there was no playground or boys running around. It was quiet and echoed and there was a lot of waiting around in a room to see him. Everyone looked miserable, including the people who worked there. Eventually we were led to a building with a long, dark corridor. A room was unlocked and there we found Michael sitting on a bed.

He was given permission to go with us to the common room. Along the way, I was my usual chatty self but feeling disheartened by Michael's lack of reply. He seemed in a dark, sullen mood. The entire atmosphere was depressing and uncomfortable, then it suddenly took a turn for the worse.

There was a commotion at the end of the hall; I looked up to see a boy of about ten years of age, shouting and striding towards us aggressively. Two men came running after him and the boy began to run. His escape ended quickly with one of the men tackling him to the floor. The other man began to strike him brutally with a big thick belt before the boy was picked up, slung over his shoulder and carried away screaming hysterically.

I was terrified and clung tightly to Dad, just wanting to get out of there. When I kept crying, Dad had to cut the visit short and take me home, but the scene was forever branded upon my mind. I had nightmares about that boy for many nights and couldn't bring myself to go back to Windana again. Dad had to continue the visits alone and I continued to write letters. Below is one Michael's replies, dated 1st August 1970

Dear Mum Dad and Storm. I hop you all are feeling well. I Love you all Please don't forget to write back.

Storm
I liked your Letter on Saturday I got my tooth out. I think I no the answer to y[our] Joke pick up your crumbs. The answer my Joke that you wrote is correct.

Mum
I hope you ate the minties I gave Last Sunday. I am thinking of you e[very] night in bed and I hope that you are th[inking] of me too.

Dad.
I am glad that you are visiting me sunday. I Love you Dad.

Yours truely
Michael Taylor

x x x x x x x x

I can't imagine what my parents suffered, knowing he was in that place. They considered any physical discipline to be abusive and cruel, and couldn't understand why anyone would want to hurt a child.

At school, there was always the threat of corporal punishment and I saw several incidents of highly abusive treatment of children by teachers. It always terrified me, but Mum would constantly assure me it would never happen to me, as if she knew something I didn't.

As a well-behaved child, getting the highest grades possible on all my schoolwork, there was no reason for me to be disciplined. The day I did get into trouble, it was for some bizarre rule applied by a new female teacher. We both suffered for her actions that day.

I'd made the mistake of leaving the lunch shed before she had dismissed us. She came after me and smacked me several times, marched me across the yard and made me stand against the wall opposite the shed, where everyone could see me.

I had never once suffered any instance of corporal punishment and I was distraught, frightened and rapidly becoming hysterical. Michael had seen it all and immediately came to my rescue, ignoring the teacher shouting at him to return to the shed. Instead he came to me, hugged me and begged me to hold on while he ran home to get Mum.

When the teacher finally dismissed me, I went to the toilets and curled up under a sink, shaking and sobbing so much I was unable to speak to my friends who were trying to comfort me. Children came to look at me, and before long my mother arrived. My friends rushed out to bring her to me, sensing something was about to happen.

I remember being gathered into her arms and held while her strong, port-flavoured breath wafted over me. It took her a long time before she was able to coax me out of the toilet block through a crowd of kids watching in fascination. When she did, it all escalated rather quickly. Outside, the doomed teacher made the grave mistake of approaching us, and Michael was quick to point her out as the culprit.

Mum handed me over to Michael before striding up to the teacher and smacking her right in the face. The teacher shrank back and wilted in shock under the verbal attack which followed. Michael and I watched in awe with every other stupefied child in the playground. At this stage, the deputy headmaster came running into the fray and I was momentarily fearful Mum might cop it herself.

Mr. Elliott was a tall, scary man, a terror to every student and teacher in the school. I'd seen him mete out harsh corporal punishment to the boys in our class. The girls were terrified enough by his fierce, icy glare. Oddly, he always spoke and acted kindly towards me, occasionally gracing me with a rare smile. The first year he became my teacher I was just as frightened of him as everyone else, but I soon came to realise it was different for me.

What he did at that moment still mystifies me. He got between the women and quietly calmed Mum down before turning to the teacher with that deathly glare.

"You're mistaken. Storm is not a child who gets into trouble."

The teacher crumbled and nodded silently before awkwardly excusing herself. Mr Elliott remained and listened politely as my drunken mother, over a foot shorter than him, continued her threats toward any bastard who would dare touch her child.

I am still perplexed by what happened that day. It makes me wonder if Mr Elliott was concerned for my welfare at home. Although Mum and Dad rarely attended school functions or teacher meetings, much to my relief, there had been other times when my inebriated parents had visited the school. Dad hid it well, but Mum was always a little too loud and embarrassing, attracting disapproving glances from other parents and titters from my class mates. Whatever the reason, it was a good outcome. Mum didn't end up in prison and the teacher didn't quit. She was even quite nice to me after that which was surprising too.

A year or so later, Mr Elliott became my teacher and still treated me very differently from most of the other children. I was appointed his monitor and often sent to do jobs for him. By then, I had become best friends with a girl in my class. Diane was the youngest of seven children and our fathers were childhood friends. My privileges then extended to her.

In our final year at primary school, Mr Elliott brought us into the smoke-filled staffroom and told the teachers he wanted us to take over the tea duties. There was no objections, and every school day during that year Diane and I were excused from the lesson before lunchtime so we could make the pot of tea and set out the cups, saucers and ashtrays in the staffroom.

Mostly, I have good memories of my primary school years, but for Michael it was just another institution. He hated strict authority and anything which demanded conformity or impeded upon his freedom. As a child, I had no understanding of why he did things which would inevitably have him locked up again.

It was another forty years before I discovered how evil these places had been. In 2004, a government inquiry was launched into the horrific sexual and physical abuse which had occurred in many of the South Australian institutions responsible for 'reforming' children. The final report came out in 2008, and I ploughed through case after case looking for any reference to Michael.

I could only conclude that it was impossible for him to have escaped repeated abuse by staff and older boys, not that I'd had any doubts. I'd seen the change in him. Most of his soul had been destroyed in Glandore. After Windana he was a shell of the happy little boy he had been. All the adventures were gone along with his hopes and dreams for the future. His life had become about surviving.

Through the years that followed, Michael was only at home for short periods. Most of the time I felt like an only child. The loneliness ate at me, especially on weekends when my parents were drinking. Diane often stayed over; I was grateful to have a friend who was unperturbed by my drunken parents.

By the age of ten, I had found a new philosophy to deal with their habits: if you can't beat them, join them. I hated everything about the taste and smell of their port, but I quite liked beer and the way it made me feel light-hearted after a few glasses. My parents saw nothing wrong with me having a drink with them on the weekend.

I'd also taken an interest in horseracing and was soon using my pocket money to gamble. On Saturday mornings, Dad and I would discuss everything about the horses racing, their jockeys and trainers, and the conditions of the tracks, before going to the betting shop to place our bets. The afternoons would be spent with my parents listening to the races on the radio, while having a beer and a chat. If we did well, Dad and I would often take another trip to the betting shop to put some more money on the trotters.

I often did well, and Dad gave me lectures on responsible gambling as the money came in. He never interfered in how I gambled but he had a strict rule about losing. If I lost my money, there was no compensation. Oddly enough, it taught me about quitting while ahead and soon I had a tin stuffed with money.

It went a long way to becoming independent at an early age, being able to buy the things I wanted like records and trips to the movies with Mum. Weekends weren't as lonely anymore and I loved these years with my parents.

They became open to talking about our family. As I approached my teens, my curiosity was increasing about the circumstances surrounding my adoption. I particularly wanted to know where Robin fitted into the picture.

Mum explained she had been married to someone else before Dad, and Robin was her eldest child from that marriage. There was another child, her daughter Kathleen, who was seven years younger. I was aware of Kathleen but only from the large portrait which had always sat on Mum's dresser, depicting a pretty blonde girl with a ribbon in her hair.

The only other child attached to our family was the little boy, Wayne Lawrence Taylor, whom my parents had lost at a few days old. Even after all those years, I could see the pain in their faces whenever they spoke of him,

Inevitably, the question of my birth father came up, but my parents claimed to be uncertain of who he was. At that time it didn't occur to ask them anything about Susan. I had assumed she was from Aunty Margaret's doomed marriage. Susan had two much older siblings, Helen and Phillip. I had often heard Dad and Aunty Margaret talking about them at Grandma's house, but I had only ever seen them once during a Christmas visit. It occurred to me they were also my siblings but I felt no need to pursue this.

For the time being, my curiosity was satisfied and I was surviving without Michael's companionship. There were still plenty of Sundays when Dad and I went to visit him in whatever institution he was residing in, and I still wrote letters every week.

Spending time with Dad went a long way to combatting my loneliness. We had horseraces, books and movies in common, and on school holidays I hung out at his pub in the city. In a smoke-fogged front bar, I learned to play pool and sat around listening to the yarns of patrons, absorbing everything and observing weird and wonderful people. I was popular with his customers and always had a drink, a ham sandwich and a bag of chips in front of me.

Sometimes the customers brought in bags of books and would let me go through them. I had been reading from the age of two and through the years had devoured all sorts of stories. Many of them were way beyond my years, having very adult themes, but there was no censorship at all in my home.

Newspapers added to my education. I read them daily and followed some of the horrific crimes occurring through the seventies in South Australia, including accounts of children who had gone missing. Rather than frighten me, it made me aware of the devious nature of people and how vulnerable children were. I vowed never to fall prey to anyone.

Dad and I enjoyed reading and watching Westerns. One of our favourite series of books was by the authors J. T. Edson and Jake Logan. They were great adventure stories meant for adults, containing sexual themes and violence, which went a long way to educating me about life. By the age of twelve, I knew exactly where babies came from and how they were made.

Sex really interested me and I wanted to know more about it. Having my own money, it was easy to buy adult magazines from the city newspaper stands. At these busy outlets nobody took much notice of a young girl throwing a couple of porn magazines in with a newspaper or two. It was just a matter of slapping the money down with a grunt about keeping the change. This extracurricular reading was kept hidden from my parents knowing they did have limits.

The pictures fascinated me, but the stories which readers sent in were even more informative, using explicit language to relate their tales of weird and wonderful exploits and fetishes. It didn't shock me or incite me to indulge in anything I was seeing or reading. To me, it was just the same as learning about any other subject which interested me.

The education these books and magazines provided gave me more than just an early understanding of my body and the changes which were taking place. It gave me an insight into relationships, and that sex didn't have to be confined to marriage or even to commitment. It could be done for fun and not just for procreation. Sex was awesome and one day I would look forward to trying it out, but I was in no hurry.

My increasing knowledge about all aspects of life was something I kept to myself after an incident at school. In my final year at primary school, we were assigned the task of writing a story and illustrating it. I wrote my first erotic romance and drew a picture of a couple engaged in a passionate kiss.

The first I knew anything was wrong was when Mr Elliott asked to see me at lunchtime. He wasn't angry, but said my story was well written and my picture was good, but it had caused some worry among the teachers. Apparently, my story had been passed around the staff room and every teacher had read it.

"I've given you full marks, but it's probably best you don't write stories like this one," he advised. "Are there books like your story at home?"

I immediately sensed trouble. "No. I saw this picture in a magazine and tried to imagine what had happened to make this couple kiss like that."

He accepted my answer because I had indeed taken my inspiration from a famous painting which he was familiar with. There was nothing further said, but I was determined not to draw attention to myself. For the sake of peace, I behaved like any other eleven year-old and shared my secrets with no one.

At some stage during the early seventies the rift between my parents, Grandma and Aunty Margaret had ended and our visits to the house resumed. With Michael gone, Susan was nicer to me but I still wasn't ready to tell her about our real relationship to each other. I had learned the importance of keeping things to myself, while silently observing and listening to the conversations. Bit by bit, I was piecing together the secrets about my family.

CHAPTER SEVEN

1975

As I approached my teenage years I despised being treated like a child. I was confident and self-assured, something which came in handy when I started high school. I had elected to go to an all-girls school, mainly because Diane would be going there. Mum and Dad liked it because it boasted of being progressive and had abolished corporal punishment.

On my first day I was mortified to learn Diane and I wouldn't be in the same class. I was in a room with girls I didn't know, who were already friends with each other. The structure was very different from primary school; I had a new teacher and classroom for every subject. There was none of the nurturing environment of primary school.

By lunchtime I was feeling agitated and contemplating going home. Instead, I decided to visit Diane in her classroom next to the library. At the door I was met by a girl who was taller than me and determined to stop me from entering.

"You're not allowed in here," she said. "Go back to your own classroom."

"I've come to see my friend," I explained.

She mockingly echoed my words and started making fun of me, much to the amusement of the girls with her. I tried to reason with her but she only got more aggressive and pushed me back out into the foyer which led to the library.

The moment she lay hands on me, my temper exploded. I grabbed her arm and launched her up against the full length window. She gasped in shock and became frightened as my hand went to her throat and held her. I leaned in towards her face and whispered through gritted teeth, using some of the expletives I knew so well.

"Don't fucking mess with me and I won't have to hurt you."

I released her and watched her dissolve in tears. When I turned to walk away I saw more girls had gathered and were watching in horrified fascination. They looked at me with mouths hanging open. No one said a word as I walked away.

For the rest of the day I awaited the summons to the principal's office but it never came. At the end of the day I went home feeling very unhappy about returning to school. The next morning, I met Diane on the bus and she said the girls had been talking about it, but she hadn't heard them say anything bad about me.

I wasn't convinced and entered my classroom warily, ready to fight anyone who wanted to badmouth me.

Instead, many of the girls began to talk to me and make me welcome among their circles. I wasn't particularly wanting any other friend than Diane, but through my three short years at high school I moved between the groups, from the nerdy girls to the rebels.

Teachers were another dynamic. Either I liked them, co-operated and did well in class, or I disliked them and made their jobs a little harder. I wouldn't allow anyone to talk down to me and demanded as much respect as the teachers themselves wanted.

There were only a few teachers who regretted going up against me. One of them was a man. I disliked him from the outset, with his mullet hairstyle, his Burt Reynolds moustache and tight shorts. He took our class for geography and his attitude towards girls infuriated me. He'd often made remarks which inferred that girls were brainless and more interested in talking, make-up and clothes.

I would answer him back with a quick-witted or sarcastic remark which made the girls laugh. One day he got aggressive, throwing a piece of chalk across the classroom and telling me he was sick of my smart mouth. Then he made the mistake of threatening me.

"It's a pity they don't use corporal punishment in this school or you might think twice about opening your mouth."

I scoffed and replied in a deliberately sultry tone. "Yes, I'm sure you'd like that, wouldn't you, Sir... me bent over your desk."

I watched him turn pale and heard the collective gasp from my fellow students. He flustered for a moment before walking out the room. Half an hour later I received the summons to the principal's office.

The school counsellor was waiting for me. She was a hard, gruff woman but I liked her and was fairly certain she was in a relationship with the principal. I was given a lecture about respecting my teachers but it wasn't given with any enthusiasm. I suspect the counsellor had been amused by this particular teacher being put in his place and I was dismissed without consequences.

Beyond the confines of school, my worldly education was continuing and Michael had come back into my life. He was sixteen that year, and instead of coming home he moved into a flat with some friends.

I think my parents had encouraged this. By then, Mum and Dad had dealt with enough and didn't like the idea of Michael being home and around me at such a vulnerable age. His flat was only a few streets away and I would use the excuse of walking our fox terrier, Tess, to visit Michael and his dog, Herman - a scrawny, over-excited kelpie-cross who seemed as much in need of affection as his owner. Herman was twice as big as Tess, but my feisty fox terrier quickly established who was boss.

Michael had other friends who weren't as nice as Herman. They were older and had tattoos and long hair, much like the music artists of that era whose heavy rock music was always loudly playing throughout my visits.

There was drug paraphernalia littering the coffee table and the cigarettes they passed around had a weird aroma. From the books I had read, I was already familiar with marijuana and the joints and water bongs they had. I wanted to try it.

Michael strongly objected but got badgered and outvoted by his friends who thought it amusing to get a young kid stoned. The first time I tried it, I remember doing a lot of coughing and nothing much else after that, except walking home in the late afternoon with Michael angry at me. He'd had to wait until I was straight enough to keep our parents from knowing what I'd been up to.

Soon after he came around home with Herman to say he was moving elsewhere. For the first time in a very long time, I enjoyed an afternoon like days gone by. Mum and Dad didn't even question where Michael had got the car which was parked out front. We all knew it was stolen, but being together was more important for all of us.

We were going to have dinner together, but Michael said he needed to go to the shop. He didn't come back. Somehow it was expected, but I was still disappointed, knowing it might be a long time before I saw him again. The one compensation was the gift he had left behind. Herman became part of our family, much to Tess's disapproval, though they eventually became the best of friends.

Sometime later, I got a letter from Michael saying he was living with his girlfriend. I finally accepted my fun times with Michael were over. He wouldn't be coming home again. There would be no more games or adventures, no getting up in the middle of the night to cook pancakes or lying in his bed to talk.

As sad as it was, Michael's absence was easier to accept with the life I had at the time. I had Diane and we were having our own adventures. I had Herman and Tess, and was enjoying the weekends with Mum and Dad. If they passed out early I would simply take my dogs to the park and stay there long into the night.

As my first year of high school ended I was looking forward to holidays and Christmas. Robin was with us, and I was even optimistic about Grandma, Aunty Margaret and Susan visiting for the first time in years. I was getting on well with Susan, and without Michael with us that year it was good to have someone my own age enjoying the day with me.

I truly believed it would be a wonderful time without any repeat of the disastrous Christmas of 1968. Surely the adults had learned a lesson and we could get through one day together without fighting. I now know my hopes were unachievable given the bitter history each of them had with the other, made worse by their dependency on alcohol to soothe wounds. Nobody ever stayed sober enough to hold a conversation which might have finally put the past to rest.

My hope for a pleasant Christmas Day was dashed by mid-afternoon when the booze began flowing liberally and the volume of their voices had gone up a notch. I wallowed in condescending fury towards these stupid adults who couldn't figure out that alcohol was the problem. If I could see it, as young as I was, why couldn't they?

This time I was older, curious and determined to listen to what they were arguing about. While spending time with Susan in my bedroom, I made frequent silent visits to the refrigerator which was stationed beside the door leading to the kitchen, where the adults were gathered. My and Susan's names were mentioned several times. Dad and Robin were telling the women to shut up and leave the past in the past, but they weren't having much success.

"You should have faced up to your responsibilities," Grandma was screeching. "But you were as bad as your mother, that black bitch from Birkenhead."

"You, you old cow," Mum was yelling back. "You had no business sticking your nose into it. We had talked about it. We'd made an agreement and had the adoption underway. I had everything ready for her: the crib, all the clothes I knitted... and then you got into Margaret's head and fucked it all up."

Aunty Margaret was crying. "Leave Mum alone. It was my decision."

"Bullshit, you've always let that old bitch boss you about. She would have been better off with us than living in that hovel full of cat shit you're raising her in."

Grandma came back at her. "Mind your own fucking business. What has your son ever done while Margaret's worked her arse off without any help from him?"

"I tried to help." Robin stated. "But I was told to stay away and keep my nose out of it, to stick my money up my arse. I wasn't allowed to do anything, or even see her. You didn't want me in her life."

"I didn't need anyone's help," Aunty Margaret replied. "I've managed fine on my own and we don't need your charity. Go back to Canberra and stay out of our lives."

I suddenly realised they weren't fighting about me. They were fighting about Susan. The more I heard, the more I struggled to comprehend the implications.

By then Susan was aware of the loud, drunken voices and the trouble brewing in the kitchen. Both of us knew where it was heading and the misery it threatened. I suggested removing ourselves, getting as far away as possible. If I'd been alone, I would have taken the dogs to the parklands and stayed there, but I had Susan to think about. I suggested we sit out on the front verandah. Maybe we would see our neighbours in the house attached to ours and find sanctuary.

A lovely couple, Gladys and Pete, had recently moved in with their two little boys. I had known Gladys for years, having gone to pre-school with her nieces. She was one of four Irish sisters living in Adelaide with a lot more brothers back in Ireland. She often had me over for a cup of tea and a chat. On Friday nights I babysat for her while she and Pete went to the local pub for a drink. Sometimes they had big family gatherings and I would sit in their kitchen, listening to the laughter and their wonderful Irish-accented voices loudly talking over each other.

That day the house was quiet and their big Ford station wagon wasn't parked out front. One of our neighbours was home though, the tiny elderly woman who lived across the road. Mrs Best fitted my idea of the perfect grandmother, gentle and loving to her two grandchildren whom she cared for on weekends. I was often invited to have lunch with them and would eagerly accept. I loved being there. Her fairy-tale home was filled with trinkets, lacy doilies and a constant aroma of baking. While her grandchildren had milk, Mrs Best knew I was fond of a cup of tea. She would make me one, brewed in a china teapot and served in a china teacup with saucer, spoon and napkin.

There was a bench seat out on her front verandah and I often saw Mum and Mrs Best sitting together. Sometimes Gladys would go across to join them. Dad and I had a name for this gathering.

"I see the Jaffrey Street council is in session again," Dad would say. "Nothing gets by that lot."

When Mrs Best saw Susan and me out the front, she came across to wish us a Happy Christmas. For a little while, our troubles were forgotten but were never far away. We were feeling better when the chaos inside suddenly came stumbling out the front door. Mum and Aunty Margaret were screaming at each other and Tess had followed them out, yapping furiously.

"Ladies, ladies, please..." Mrs Best was cross with them. "These girls don't need to see your nonsense."

But they were too focussed on hating each other and soon the fighting got physical again and tumbled out onto the road. Susan was crying and screaming at them to stop or she was going home. I just sank down on the verandah and cuddled Tess tightly against me and watched as Mrs. Best intervened.

This dear little woman, much older and shorter than these two banshees, bravely stepped into the fray to break it up. I feared she would get hurt, but she stood partway between them, telling them off until they finally listened to her.

By then, Grandma had come out the front, muttering and cursing. She gave me a sour look then went after Susan who was striding down the road. With a final glare at Mum, Aunty Margaret straightened her clothes and followed. Their curses and departing commentary eventually faded away. Even Mum's angry, tearful rants soon died down with Mrs Best's soothing voice.

"Come back to my house, Lilian. I'll pour you a sherry and we can chat."

"I can't." Mum looked at me, as if finally taking stock of her behaviour. "I have to look after Storm."

"Storm is fine, aren't you dear? Wally and Robin are inside."

"Yes, but I need to fix Storm some dinner soon."

47

It wasn't the time to be angry with her and I was eager to be alone. "I'm okay, Mum. Go have a drink with Mrs Best."

"Maybe just one drink."

I walked with them to the gate, and as Mrs Best helped Mum inside she gave me a concerned smile.

"I'll look after your Mum, dear. You just go and enjoy your evening and tomorrow come and have dinner with me. David and Donna will be here and I'll make us chicken and chips."

I wanted to hug her. I wanted a grandmother like Mrs Best. She was a true friend to our family, as were Gladys and Pete. What I appreciated most was how they all knew my parents' vices and made no judgements. Their homes often provided me with a haven to escape to, where I could just relax and feel the normality of sober people.

When I went home that day, Robin and Dad were still drinking and talking. I left them to it and went to my bedroom where I could think about what I had heard earlier. There was no other conclusion I could come to. Robin was Susan's father, whether it was from a night of passion or a short relationship. Knowing Robin's life in the Navy, and his residence in Canberra, I was certain it was the former.

It was difficult to comprehend and only raised more questions. Did it mean that Robin was also my father? My relationship to Robin was evolving with every new revelation, from brother to step-brother to the possibility of father. I hated it and craved the kind of families my friends had, where parents didn't get drunk and didn't have secrets.

I didn't like the idea of Robin and Margaret being together at all. She was his step-aunt and eleven years older. In my young mind they had no business being together, let alone having children. It was uncomfortable thinking I might have been born of their union as Susan had been.

On the brink of puberty, I harboured a lot of anger towards my family and was bearing the burden alone. I yearned for those nights with Michael when we could talk things over. I resented my history being kept from me and finally decided I had a right to know.

I waited for Robin to return to Canberra before confronting my parents, and I didn't hold back. I told them everything else I had learned and demanded answers.

"Is he? Is Robin my father too?"

"We don't know," Dad sighed. "We know he is Susan's father. Robin seems to think he is your father too, but we don't think he was around at the time when Aunty Margaret got pregnant with you."

"You were going to adopt Susan, weren't you?"

Mum was crying as she explained. "We wanted children so much. Aunty Margaret was going to have Robin's baby and she was still suffering from her marriage breakup. Bill had full custody of Philip and Helen. She was only allowed to see them occasionally, and with her being alone and pregnant he had more ammunition to deem her unfit. Grandma was constantly berating her for getting pregnant and it made sense for us to take the baby."

'Margaret agreed and it was all arranged. We filed papers with the courts to adopt the baby at birth. But when Susan was born we came to get her, only to be told we couldn't have her. Aunty Margaret said she had changed her mind, but she was just doing what Grandma told her to do. She was always letting herself get pushed around by Grandma."

Even all those years later I could see Mum remembering that heartbreak. Eleven years after losing their only child at a few days old, they were losing another child - one they wanted so badly and had so much to offer. They would have to endure seeing Susan growing up in Grandma's house, knowing how close she had come to being theirs.

I had got my answer, but one that left me emotionally exhausted. My other questions were forgotten, such as why Grandma hated Mum so much. Knowing the truth didn't bring me any peace. I had to decide what I wanted to do about it.

Being closer to Susan, I felt she had a right to know our true relationship. We were sisters, not cousins, but I wasn't certain how she would feel about it. After stewing about it for weeks, I took off in the middle of the night and headed to Grandma's house. I tapped on Susan's bedroom window and got her to come out the front.

"I have something to tell you, and I don't know how you're going feel about it, but I think you have a right to know."

At the age of twelve, it should never have been my burden to tell her. That night I told her everything. For the next thirty years, Susan and I tried to be sisters, but there was always an underlying resentment which caused

49

contention between us. Susan once told me I had ruined her life, and for years I had no idea what she meant. I'd never caused her any harm.

It was through the process of writing this memoir I began to wonder. Did she resent me for being the one to tell her? Would she have preferred never to know, especially about how she was the one who Mum and Dad had set out to adopt?

In the weeks which followed all hell broke loose. Grandma and Aunty Margaret confronted Mum and Dad about what I had done. Grandma made no attempt to hide her resentment towards me. I was called a nasty little bitch for sticking my nose into a matter which didn't concern me. Mum and Dad even questioned my thinking for having told Susan. I know I harboured a lot of guilt for a long time afterwards and it went a long way to filling my teenage years with anger.

We didn't see Robin the next year, but I know Mum was writing to him. I was fourteen before he visited again, and by then I was done with adults keeping things from me. As usual, Robin spent a good deal of the time taking me out and wasn't overly shocked when I confronted him.

"You think that you are my father, don't you?" I asked as we drove back from the movies.

Robin sighed. "I am your father and Susan's too, but Mum and Wally are your parents."

"I know that," I nodded. "It's just weird."

"Yeah I know. Mum's worried that you're growing up too fast. She says you don't act like a kid anymore."

"I'm not a kid anymore. I haven't felt like a kid for a long time. I'm not like kids my own age. I know things they don't."

"None of this changes how much I love you."

"I know that too and I love you, too, but you're my brother, not my Dad."

"I know, but for me, I can't help feeling that you'll always be my daughter."

He held that conviction until the day he died several weeks after his 80th birthday. Whenever I had visited him and his family in Canberra, I was considered his daughter and treated as such. I loved being part of his family and proud to be a sister to his five children.

In recent years, while researching our family tree, I had begun to suspect he was wrong. A simple DNA test would have told me the truth, but I couldn't bring myself to take it while he was still alive. He had honoured me with his pride in claiming me as his child. I returned the honour in refusing to know for certain. He died with his belief. For once, knowing the truth wasn't so important.

Robin Wilfred Duval Clifford
(1935 – 2015)

CHAPTER EIGHT

BOYS

By my third year in high school I had lost interest in all subjects except drama. The world beyond the school gates had a far more interesting education to offer. Boys were interesting and, though I wanted to experience the excitement of dating, I had no intention of getting into a relationship. I discovered early how bored I got after more than one date.

Like most girls I had some weird belief that boys knew how to take the lead, but it didn't take long to realise how little they knew. It was all bravado, putting on an act as if they had some vast knowledge about sex. I was shocked and highly amused to find out they didn't. The first time I initiated a passionate kiss the boy pulled away in horror.

He had been fine with groping me, but the moment I took the lead he wilted. Girls were supposed to be innocent, submitting to the superior wisdom of masculinity. Not that I was interested in having sex with anyone. I wanted that moment to be perfect, with the man of my choice. In the meantime I was happy to have some fun along the way.

I quickly lost interest in boys my own age and began to look at older men, where I was bound to find someone who held my interest or, at least, knew the meaning of the word 'foreplay.' Surprisingly they were hard to find, or I was looking in the wrong places. It was when I wasn't looking I had a terrifying introduction to a breed of men who wouldn't take 'no' for an answer.

One Saturday I had taken Tess and Herman to the parklands and stopped to watch the last few minutes of a hockey match. When it was over I went to walk off but was stopped by a one of the players. He was tall, attractive and at least nineteen years of age.

He struck up a conversation about my dogs and squatted down to pat them. He was friendly, interesting and easy to talk to. He introduced himself as Tony.

"We're over from Sydney and we're staying at that motel on the corner. We leave on Monday. You should come by tomorrow. We're having a few drinks in our room."

I was definitely interested. "What time?"

"Come over about four o'clock." He gave me the room number and winked at me before jogging back to his team.

My heart was racing and I could hardly wait for Sunday to arrive. This guy ticked a lot of boxes, but I also liked the prospect of hanging out with his team, having a couple of drinks and a fun time. It would be something to boast about on Monday morning at school.

I used the excuse of walking the dogs to get out the house without alerting my parents. Going to a motel room to meet a bunch of men would not have gone down well. I saw nothing wrong with it. As far as I was concerned, I was in charge of my body and fate. Who I shared physical contact with, and how far it went, would be my decision. Surely everyone respected that.

I knew about these monsters who raped girls. I'd read several accounts of sexual assault in the newspapers and books I had read, but I had naively believed the perpetrators as having something abnormal about them. The stories always foreshadowed something not quite right, or some sinister character trait. Normal people didn't do things like that, and especially charming, intelligent guys. I was about to find out how terribly wrong I was.

When I arrived at the motel there was only a few hockey players about. Apparently most of them had gone home. There certainly wasn't the party atmosphere I had expected. Tony shrugged it off. I was still interested in spending time with him, so we went to his room. Tess and Herman were happy enough, and they stretched out on the floor while Tony and I sat on the bed.

We hadn't said much when he leaned in to kiss me. I was fine with that, but when his hands started wandering I stopped him.

"No, I'm not going that far," I laughed. "I'm just here to hang out for a bit."

Tony laughed as if I'd said something ridiculous and then carried on as if I'd said nothing at all. I pushed him off.

"Hey, I said I wasn't going there. Don't do that."

He laughed again before his tactics suddenly got violent. He shoved me down on the bed and got on top of me, pinning me to the bed. It took a few seconds to comprehend what was happening. He was bigger and heavier than I was and my strength was no match for his. His weight kept me trapped while his hands ripped my shirt open.

I had never experienced fear of that magnitude as I realised how helpless I was against him. His hand was working to get my jeans off when my rescue unexpectedly arrived. Tony launched himself off of me as Herman snapped and repeatedly sank his teeth into him. I was up off the bed, pulling my jeans back in place as I watched my dogs rip into him.

I had never seen Herman vicious in the slightest, had never imagined he was capable of it until that day. Tony was kicking at them, but Herman was determined to have a piece of him. I ran to the door and screamed at them to come. Tess had been hurt and quickly obeyed but it took a bit more yelling to summon Herman back. I saw a lot of blood, and Tony dropping onto the bed making a lot of noise.

I didn't wait to ask if he was alright. I ran out of there to the carpark across the road with my dogs following. When I was certain I was safe I sank down to the ground and dissolved into hysterical crying, clutching Herman against me. He was still excited, madly licking at my face with his tail wagging furiously. Tess was barking at us so I drew her on to my lap to keep her quiet.

I did up my shirt and stayed there for a long time, shaking and fearful about a lot of things, but least about what had happened to me. My main concern was my parents finding out and Herman getting into trouble for attacking someone. I blamed myself for getting into that situation.

Only when I was certain my emotions were under control did I return home. I feigned some illness and didn't go to school for a few days, wanting to be home if the police arrived to take Herman away. During that time I pondered everything and continued blaming myself.

Tess was always a little snappy, as fox terriers often are, but Herman never showed his vicious side again. He remained the over-excited, friendly dog he'd always been, whose tail never stopped wagging and knocking things over.

A year later Herman passed away and I grieved deeply for him. For many years his heroic deed was kept locked away in my heart. I never got to tell Michael of the precious gift and friend he had given me. Guilt, shame and the attitude of society kept me silent.

Me with my two heroes Tess and Herman

In recent years, with abusive men finally being shown for what they are, I've rehashed that incident and pondered what might have happened if I'd spoken up. I concluded it would have been terrible for me. Even at fourteen the blame would have been laid on me, having gone to the motel. Herman would have probably been put down. I'm glad I didn't speak up.

Recently, in social media, there has been criticism that women have gone too far in fighting back and men are feeling victimised. I disagree.

For me, believing an adult man would respect my boundaries is neither naïve, foolish or too much to expect. Let the blame fall where it belongs - on a nineteen-year old man who was fully prepared to rape a fourteen-year old girl. He knew he would be gone the next day and unlikely to give it a second thought. My life would have been destroyed.

I carried my guilt for years and was unprepared for what the Me Too Movement would trigger in me. By then I had experienced three violent sexual assaults, one of them at the hands of a Social Security case worker when I applied for benefits.

The last one was when I was married with two young children and working as a cleaner. The police were called to that one and I was taken to the police station and made to strip my top of in an open office area crowded with people while they checked for bruises,

I was asked what I might have done to provoke the attack. I was cleaning a unit for a disabled man who had inadvertently taken on a flatmate who had just been released on parole.

I was told nothing until three months later when an officer turned up at our house to tell us Barry had pleaded guilty and been sentenced to three months for aggravated assault. The fact that I crippled him with a knee to his genitals was the only reason his crime hadn't been worse. None of that mattered and I was never offered counselling.

If 'Me Too' has incited women to aggressively take on a culture of predatory males then they have my full support. The emotional impact of my own experiences has been enormous and ongoing. The years may pass, but the feelings of terror, guilt and shame remain branded into our souls.

And I know abuse is not exclusive to girls. I will never know the extent of what my brother, along with countless other young boys suffered in institutions. I do know that by the age of twelve there was nothing left of the brother I had grown up with.

My experience of that first predatory male hardened me and darkened my attitude towards males. I had little respect for them, and often felt vengeful. Rather than be intimidated I got bolder and dressed more provocatively, as if I had some need to accentuate what they couldn't have. I became familiar with the word 'slut' being mentioned in my hearing and I wore the title proudly.

Once, while at the Parkside Hotel with Dad, men were staring at me and making dirty comments. I was dressed in a low-cut halter-neck dress with a hem which resided high up around my thighs. When one of the comments reached Dad's hearing, he stood up and glared at the man.

"That's my daughter and I'll fucking take you out if you open your fat, fucking trap again."

We were asked to leave and Dad was banned from the pub. On our way home, I felt awful and once again blamed myself.

"I'm sorry Dad. I won't wear this again."

He stopped and lit his cigarette, frowning at me. "You wear whatever you want, and anyone ever talks to you like that again, you kick them as hard as you can, right in the balls. It will drop them every time."

Mum was equally supportive when we told her what happened. She laughed. "That's just stupid men. Your dad had to put up with a lot of that when we were first together. He got into a lot of fights back then over men making remarks about me. You wear what you want."

It wasn't the first time my parents had shown their very feminist attitudes. In my fifth year at primary school in our art lesson, the boys were going to be making fruit baskets with ice-cream sticks while the girls sewed cushion covers. I wanted to make a fruit basket but the teacher refused. I complained about it to Mum.

The next morning she came in to see my teacher. "Why can't Storm make a fruit basket?"

"It's more practical for girls to do sewing."

"Why?"

The teacher couldn't say but refused to give in. We all ended up in the headmaster's office where Mum laid down the law.

"Storm doesn't want to learn to sew. She never has. She wants to make a fruit basket. Unless you can give me a better reason why she can't, she can stay home this week and I'll buy her the sticks so she can make one."

The headmaster took Mum's side and I got my way. I did her proud by making the best fruit basket and helping some of the boys with theirs. There were lots of giggles and tittering from the girls about me being with the boys, but I didn't care.

It was my parents who made me understand that women were in no way inferior to men in anything. Dad would often go further in saying women were much smarter than men. He had something else to say that day after being kicked out of the pub.

"God gave men a brain and cock, and only enough blood to use one at a time."

It was his way of telling me to be careful, but not once was any blame assigned to me. I nearly told Mum and Dad about the incident at the motel but decided against it. I didn't want them to worry about me, and I'd already made steps to protect myself.

I was venturing further from home when I could, and often went into the city on my own to see a movie. There was a cinema in Hindley Street which played unusual and art house movies which fascinated me, but attracted some ominous patrons. I carried one of Mum's hat pins in my shoulder bag and was always aware of my surroundings, determined not to be caught out again.

It was in that cinema I saw the controversial movie called the *Story of O* which had attracted an unusual audience. It was my introduction to people who openly lived in fetish lifestyles as seen in their outfits. They fascinated me, and the movie stirred something inside of me which I knew had existed for a long time, but at fourteen I had no real understanding of it. I still had a lot to learn about life and myself, but that's another story echoed in my fictional ones.

I hadn't seen much of Michael that year. He had celebrated his 18th birthday by being released from McNally Training Centre. They'd got him a job as a swimming instructor in Whyalla. It was October before I saw him again and he had a surprise for us all. With him was his girlfriend, Julie, and their beautiful baby boy, Clinton. Mum and Dad were thrilled about being grandparents and I couldn't contain my joy over having become an aunt.

Clinton looked just like his father and we all loved Julie immediately. She was bubbly and chatty and in love with my brother. Michael was a proud, doting father and I could see he was genuinely happy. It gave me hope of finally seeing Michael finding peace. For a while his family achieved that for him, but the demons of his past still tormented him. Finding lasting happiness wasn't something Michael could ever keep hold of.

I visited Michael, Julie and Clinton as often as I could, riding my bike to their flat in Dulwich. Looking after Clinton brought me enormous joy; changing his nappies, bathing him and cuddling him off to sleep. I was sure there was no greater happiness than being a mother.

It was wonderful seeing my brother enjoying family life, but it didn't last long. By Clinton's first birthday Michael was back in prison. It was daunting knowing I would have to visit him yet again in another institution, and this one was quite a distance away. It took hours by buses to get there and back, especially on a Sunday when buses didn't run frequently. In my frustration I took up the habit of hitching a lift with strangers, and soon I was hitchhiking everywhere.

Often I was picked up by families. The concerned adults would lecture me about predators and how dangerous hitchhiking was, and then go out of their way to take me all the way to my destinations. It wasn't as if I hadn't learned a lesson from the incident at the motel. Something in me needed to fight back against the fear it had incited, and I actually enjoyed putting myself in dangerous situations.

Being alone didn't bother me anymore. I'd accepted it and the freedom it gave me, but I was far too sure of myself and my ability to control a situation. I kidded myself that I was a good judge of character. Anyone I deemed suspicious would be thanked and waved on. Looking back I want to kick myself for being so stupid, but thankfully I never had a bad experience from hitchhiking.

Once, Diane reluctantly came on one of these rides with me and I sat between her and the driver. There was a moment when the driver put his hand on my leg. I calmly removed it. It was only when he dropped us off, I could see how frightened Diane was. I never took her with me again. My somewhat destructive attitude was something I didn't want to inflict on others.

Soon after my 15th birthday I discovered how easily I could get into pubs and nightclubs with just a bit of make-up and a pair of high heels. My Saturday night ventures into the parklands with my dogs was over. The city offered much more excitement.

The people I met were fascinating, but it was the gay bars where I felt most at home. It was exhilarating, drinking and having fun with guys who didn't see me as something to grope. They were caring and watched over me, knowing I was far too young to be there. One night they took me to a nightclub and I was taken backstage to meet a couple of the performers.

I sat in a dressing room and watched men turn into women, fascinated as they taped their genitals up between their legs. Some of them had begun hormones or gender reassignment, which had given them a beautiful pair of breasts. Years later I met the owner of the nightclub at that time and discovered I had been with members of the world-famous Les Girls Revue.

Inevitably my parents discovered what I was doing. They were upset at first, but knew much of the blame lay with themselves and there was little they could do. It was far too late to start instilling discipline and laying down the law. I was too independent and used to making my own decisions. They decided compromise was the best solution.

We hashed out some rules we all agreed on, especially about drinking too much and leaving myself vulnerable. I didn't tell them I had been hitchhiking, but readily accepted the condition of always catching taxis wherever I went. After a long and calm conversation, Dad gave me the key to the front door and his heartfelt request.

"Always come home, no matter what."

Mum added her own. "There's nothing you can't talk to us about. If you're worried about anything, talk to us."

She meant it. In months to come, she was there for me when I had sunk to my lowest and found myself in more trouble than I could handle. Through it all there was never any condemnation or anger or demands to stop what I was doing. They knew better. My parents had an incredible solution to handling rebellious teenagers: a good sense of humour, unconditional love and a shoulder to cry on.

Their trust in me inspired a need to demonstrate how grown-up I was. I governed myself wisely, not drinking too much, politely and firmly declining the array of drugs on offer and generally keeping myself safe. I was taught a painful lesson the first time I compromised my principles.

After going to a local pub one night with friends, I realised I had drunk far too much and needed to be home. I went out onto the street to get some fresh air and saw a bus coming along. I hailed it and the bus pulled over and let me on.

During the ride I fell asleep. When I awoke, still very inebriated, the bus was pulling up at a stop in the city. I decided to get off and check out a pub I knew of down Rundle Mall. I staggered past a group of older girls and one made a sneering remark.

I stopped and turned back. "If you think I'm bothered by you fucking whores, think again."

Huge mistake. That night I got the hiding of my life - punched, kicked and slapped continually until I was bruised and bleeding. I made it worse by getting in a few punches of my own. Every time I went down I got up again and egged them on with a few more choice words. Eventually, I got the idea of staying down.

I had the sense to get a taxi home. The driver left me in the taxi and got Dad out of bed. Mum was calling out from the bedroom as Dad helped me in.

"What's going on, Wally? Is Storm alright?"

"She's fine. Go back to sleep, love. I'm just making Storm a cup of tea."

There was no way he was going to let Mum see me in that condition. He took me down to the kitchen and sat me down, examining the wounds he could see. By then the pain had set in and I was crying.

"They beat me up, Dad. These fucking bitches beat the shit out of me."

"No use bawling," he huffed. "And don't swear like that. How much fucking booze did you drink? I can smell it on your breath."

He fetched a bowl of water and antiseptic and started treating my wounds as he gave me a mild lecture.

"Your mother is going to go berserk when she sees you, you know that don't you?"

I nodded.

"That's fucking unfair on her. You need to pull your head in a bit, girl. You carry on like that, you'll get a lot fucking worse happening. Is that what you want?"

"No, Dad."

"Then fucking learn from this."

"I will, Dad."

"Now I have to stay up all night to keep an eye on you."

"You don't have to."

"Yeah, I do. I'm putting you on the couch."

Dad watched over me the entire night. He held the bucket when I awoke throwing up, and continually applied cold flannels to my face. But there was no sympathy when I cried, and I was fine with that. He wasn't about to coddle me over stupidity.

Mum was livid when she saw me in the morning and even Dad got told off.

61

"Why didn't you get me up? You said she was alright."

I was quick to jump to Dad's defence. "I'm alright, Mum. Dad fixed me up and I'm just a bit sore."

Mum was terribly upset and I was furious with myself. The pain was awful. My face and body were bruised for days. With sobriety came the awful realisation of how much worse it could have been. It scared me enough to end my nights in the city for a while, much to my parents' relief.

They had enough to deal with. After 27 years as manager of the Hotel Richmond, Dad was made redundant when the Richmond Hotel changed hands. They wanted a new look and a much younger staff. By then he was 58, and two years short of getting his war pension.

His stubborn pride wouldn't allow him to get unemployment benefits, insisting his severance pay-out would be enough to survive on. For a long time I had no idea how tightly my parents were managing their money, or how stubborn my father could be. Mum was already in her sixties and could have been getting the age pension, but Dad was determined to be seen as the provider for his family.

Mum had always let Dad handle the finances, and up until then he'd never let her down. Meanwhile, my school was offering students an expensive two-week holiday to Queensland. I wasn't particularly interested, but when I told my parents Dad said I should go. Maybe he wanted the time alone with Mum, but it came when they could least afford it, not that I knew that.

The worry was causing another problem. With Dad home, my parents had taken up drinking heavily during the week. Coming home from school to find them drunk made me angry and steered my thoughts towards moving out of home and total independence.

On weekends I worked part-time at a rest home, I'd got the job after lying about my age. It was only a few hours in the afternoon washing dishes, but one night I was asked to help out with the nurses due to a shortage of staff. After that I was made a nurse assistant caring for the elderly.

With a wage and the money I was accumulating from the races, I was already financially independent. Dad still insisted on paying for my trip to Queensland along with spending money. It was a fabulous holiday, but I came back to absolute bedlam.

Grandma's house had burned down while I was away. A kerosene heater had been knocked over. Aunty Margaret had been lauded as a hero on the front page of the newspaper, having rescued Grandma from the flames. Many of the cats hadn't been as fortunate. It all got much worse when it was revealed the house was uninsured.

They had to accept a housing trust in Findon, a suburb which required two long bus rides to get to. A local church took advantage of their distress and offered them $6000 for the property. Grandma accepted it and sold off the house for a pittance of what it was worth.

My parents had obviously helped with the financial burden, because soon I was made aware of their financial struggle. While visiting Mrs Best, I heard Mum crying and telling her they had no income left and couldn't pay the bills.

Mrs Best was insistent. "Lilian, stop this nonsense and go get your pension. You're entitled to it."

"Wally doesn't want me to do that."

"Wally needs to get off his high horse and be sensible."

The next day I went to see Mrs Best and she told me how broke they were. I asked how to go about getting Mum her pension. Later that week I took Mum to Social Security, filled out the forms and got her pension started. They back-paid the three years she'd been entitled to.

Dad wasn't happy, but at least they could pay their bills. Having solved this situation for them my mind was made up about something else I had been contemplating. School was just a nuisance and offered nothing I was interested in learning, certainly nothing to do with life.

I applied for my first full-time job, writing the application letter myself and sending it off. A week later a letter came requesting an interview in the city. The job was for a sales assistant in one of the local stores in a chain of clothing boutiques.

A few days prior I had bought an outfit from their store and I wore it to the interview. My make-up and hair were done perfectly. I was confident and said all the right things. A week later I received another letter saying my application had been successful.

Mum and Dad were stunned, but sensed it was no use arguing about it. Dad grumbled a bit that I would have to start paying board, but I was fine with that. It fitted in well with what I'd been trying to achieve. At fifteen, I was supporting myself and had complete independence. There was only one other thing I needed to fulfil my life. I wanted a baby.

CHAPTER NINE

A YEAR OF LIVING DANGEROUSLY

My job lasted a few months before I was made redundant. Termination came without warning, stating in a letter that the store was closing down and my position wasn't financially viable. I was furious, having been led to believe I had a long, prosperous career ahead of me.

During my short working life I had stopped going to the city at night and was living a busy but quieter life. Without a job I had too much time on my hands and no clear direction of what I wanted to do. I was too young to get unemployment benefits and my former position at the rest home had been filled.

I scoured the newspapers, but there was nothing which appealed to me. Mum and Dad told me not to stress about it and just spend some time relaxing. It was their hope I would consider going back to school, but they didn't harass me about it.

An entertainment venue with pinball machines had opened in a nearby suburb and I began to hang out there whenever it was open. It was a good place to meet boys, but after dating a few of them my opinion hadn't changed. I was more interested in the older men who worked at the venue.

They were in their late twenties and married, which didn't stop them showing interest in me. I was flattered by the attention. One day one of their friends showed up. My heart skipped a beat and I felt flustered by the sight of this man, Jack. He was ten years older than me and into martial arts. He was fit and muscled, attractive and single.

For the first time I felt the stirrings of desire to be with a man - this man. For a while I was happy to observe him in his position as door security. It soon became obvious I wasn't the only one attracted to him. There were always girls hanging around talking to him and I felt the stirrings of jealousy.

Luke, the owner of the venue, was friendly with me and had noticed my interest in Jack. He warned me off.

"You don't want to go there, love. Jack is a womaniser and he'll screw you and dump you within the hour."

I scoffed. "I'm not looking to marry him. Nothing wrong with a bit of fun."

Luke smiled, staring straight into my eyes. "You don't need him if it's some fun you're looking for.'

I was stunned, knowing Luke was married. I liked him but hadn't even considered any sort of relationship with him beyond the boundaries of friendship. I laughed it off as a joke and went about my business, but couldn't clear my head over what had been suggested. Worse still was my lack of disdain for such a horrid proposition.

The prospect of an affair with a married man excited me. It offered the danger I loved and a chance to try sex without commitment. I'd read enough adult novels to believe forbidden sex was often the best. In the end, the dying embers of my morality won out and I backed off. Besides, my sixteenth birthday was approaching and it seemed right to wait until then.

A crowd from the venue gathered Friday nights at the pub down the road and I tagged along. There was a nightclub directly across the road, a strip joint, and many of us patronised it after a few drinks. Jack, Luke and his best friend Steve were always there. I liked all three of them, but my heart was settled on Jack.

Apart from the occasional grin and a wink he showed little interest in me. I dated several boys from the venue, but only ever once. Some were satisfied with being friends. I knew I had a reputation and wasn't popular among the girls, but I had one good friend, Anne.

One night at the pub I stumbled on Anne and Steve making out in the car park. Anne was mortified at being caught out with a married man, but I laughed it off. Rather than bother me, I felt a little jealous.

Out the blue, Luke offered me a job at the venue and I was thrilled to be employed once again. It also allowed me to hang out there as much as I wanted. On my sixteenth birthday we all went to the pub and the strip club to celebrate. I was on top of the world once again, employed and having an awesome social life.

A few weeks later Jack approached me at work. My heart was thumping when he smiled at me.

"I was wondering if you'd like to go out to dinner and a dance with me."

I struggled to keep a cool head and stuttered some kind of acceptance.

The time beforehand seemed to drag on forever and suddenly he was there at my house, picking me up in his yellow panel van. He even chatted with Dad.

That first date was magical. We talked over dinner, danced late into the night and then he drove me home, stealing a kiss before I went inside. I was shocked by my own excitement. Had I really found a guy who I liked, who I desperately wanted to date again?

The next day at work Luke was moody and kept making snide remarks. Eventually I demanded to know what was up with him.

"I told you to stay away from Jack. He's no good and he's only after one thing."

I was furious. It didn't matter an iota that he was my boss. "It's none of your business. I'll date whoever I want. What are you going to do, sack me?"

Luke backed off and, as I suspected, wasn't about to let me go.

A week later I visited Diane for a well overdue catch-up. She was stunned by what I had been up to and revealed that she was in a relationship. Being with her again, in her home, stirred memories of just being a kid, something I hadn't felt in a long time. I remember a lot about that night, including feeling incredibly emotional and wanting to turn back the clock.

During the evening we headed to the shop to get munchies. Halfway down the road we heard loud music and the grunt of a powerful engine. My heart raced as I watched Jack pull over in his yellow panel van.

He leaned over and wound down the window. "I just called by your place and your folks said you were out. I just drove down this way to see if I could spot you."

I introduced Diane and asked what he wanted.

"I thought you and I could get a drink together, but your friend is welcome too."

We knew he was just being polite and Diane nudged me. "Go on. I know you want to."

I did. I wanted another date with Jack to see where this was heading. I even considered the possibility of a relationship. Sometimes I wish Diane had demanded we stick to our plans, but she didn't. I bid her goodbye as I climbed into the van.

Jack drove us out quite a distance to a pub and once again we had a great night talking and dancing. He asked if I wanted to go back to his place which wasn't far away. By then I had made my decision of where the night was headed.

I was nervous, but my mind was made up. Within several minutes of arriving at his place, we were in the bedroom. Things moved quickly and we were soon stripped off and under the sheets. Jack was immediately on top of me but I stopped him.

"Don't be so eager. This is my first time and I don't want to rush it."

Jack laughed. "Yeah sure. You're telling me you're a virgin."

"What about it?"

"Virgins don't act like this."

"Like what?"

He shook his head and began to initiate a little foreplay, but nothing like I'd imagined. I suggested a couple of things and he shook his head.

"No, I'm not into that. So you're not exactly a shy virgin, are you? How about you just let me take the lead?"

I knew he was mocking me and intimidated by my directness, but I was horny and had hopes things might improve during the act itself. It didn't. In a few thrusts, he was inside me and our wild romp was over in less than a minute. He rolled over and lay panting beside me, while I lay there fuming.

"How was that?"

It wasn't worth commenting about. "Great."

It was when he saw the blood on the sheets he looked at me aghast. "You actually were a virgin?"

"Yeah, well I'd better get home. Would you call me a cab?"

It was a long ride home and I was furious. I had given up my virginity for a couple of minutes of really bad sex. It confirmed everything I had suspected. For all their boasting of sexual prowess, men were liars. They either had no idea what to do or didn't care.

It occurred to me that we'd had unprotected sex, but it didn't bother me. I didn't consider getting pregnant as being anything bad, but more in line of what I wanted.

As for Jack, I chalked up the experience as another miserable lesson in life. I still liked him and had been comfortable getting intimate with him.

Maybe I would go there again. Besides, I didn't need a man to achieve a climax. The whole night was best forgotten, but that didn't happen.

A few days later, Luke bailed me up at work again. "You slept with Jack? I warned you not to go there."

I couldn't believe what I was hearing. "He told you?"

"He fucking told everyone and not very nicely. He said you were a proper slut."

My world came crashing down around me. Luke calmed down when he saw how devastated I was. He took me for a drive and I told him everything, including how useless Jack had been.

"You know," he said. "I told you if you wanted some fun you didn't need him. There are guys who know what they're doing."

I didn't want to hear that from him and got him to take me home. When Friday night came, Jack was at the pub and made no effort to talk to me. There were snide comments made all night and I eventually asked Luke to take me home. My emotions were raw.

Before we got there, I asked him to pull over. "No commitment, no pressure, just a fucking good time."

Luke nodded and headed to an empty car park. I spent the next few hours experiencing everything I had wanted, while constantly aware of how wrong it was. The last glowing embers of decency had finally gone out.

* * * * *

It didn't take long to realise Luke expected me to be exclusive to him. He got mad as I continued to date other guys. We had fights about it, where I reminded him he had a wife whom he had no intention of leaving.

Meanwhile Anne was still in a relationship with Steve and the four of us sometimes went out together. At work I'd often seen Steve having heated arguments with his wife, Kay. I wondered if she knew about Anne. Kay was also good friends with Luke's wife, Joan.

Luke always seemed the loving husband to Joan. He assured me that they had an open marriage and she was aware of his extra-marital affairs. I hadn't noticed anything which indicated she knew anything about me. Often, he would pour on his husbandly affection in front of me in hopes of making me jealous. It didn't bother me at all. I was happy to believe their marriage was unaffected by what we were doing. It was Luke's possessive attitude which annoyed me.

One night after an argument with him, I got Steve to take me home. We stopped along the way and he talked a lot about how unhappy he was in his marriage. One thing led to another and soon we were indulging our passions.

I had some conscience about cheating on Luke with his best friend. The next day I tried to end it with Luke, but he got too distraught. I agreed to stay in a relationship but suggested we back off a little at least. It was getting far too intense and I was lying to everyone, including myself. I made up excuses to go straight home after work and avoided being alone with him.

Meanwhile Steve and I continued to get together, but it didn't take long for Luke to get suspicious. I still tried to push the fact that we were in this for fun, but he was far too invested in me. Steve was much more relaxed about our situation. He talked about getting out of his marriage and staying single for the rest of his life.

It was Anne who eventually caught us. She was devastated. In the weeks which followed I had to face up to what I had done. As the consequences unfolded, I began to take a long hard look at myself.

Luke was made aware of the situation rather quickly and his response was coldly calculated. He knew if it all came out his own marriage would end. He got me alone to unleash a vicious verbal attack upon me and make quite clear I knew what he expected from me.

"Steve and I have talked. He's wanted to break up with Kay for years and he's fine if this gets out. You just make quite sure I'm not dragged into it. If I had my way you'd be out of here because I never want to see you again, but sacking you would only raise suspicions. You just do as you're told and stay the fuck away from me."

I was too disgusted with myself to understand I was being set up as the scapegoat. All I wanted to do was make it right and not be the cause of Luke's marriage ending in divorce. It was up to me to bear the brunt of it so no one else would get hurt. I continued to show up for work, trying to keep my head down, but all around me trouble was brewing.

It began with Steve telling his wife of having an affair with me, using me to end his marriage. It also diverted the attention away from Luke and the

70

blame was laid solely at my feet. Suddenly, everyone knew and my punishment was underway. The snide remarks, the blatant condemnations and nasty remarks were directed at me alone. Luke and Steve sorted their differences quickly and carried on, their friendship unaffected.

Anne took her revenge by fuelling the rumours about me. I had strangers commenting openly about what a slut I was, but I refused to retaliate. As far as I was concerned I had earned every remark. One time, an old friend of Luke and Steve's called in to see them. On passing by as I worked, he stopped and ogled me.

"Hey love, how about you and me catch up later? I've heard you're a real fucking whore in the sack." He grabbed his crotch. "I've got something that might satisfy you."

In my horror, I slapped him but his face darkened with fury. He backhanded me brutally, sending me crashing to the floor. Steve and Luke said nothing and the three of them went on their way. For the next hour I sat on the floor in the bathroom. My mouth was bleeding and I was trembling violently, and still telling myself I deserved it.

After work I went to Diane's house, but she wasn't home. I wandered down to the park and sat down on the banks of the creek, feeling as if I didn't have a friend in the world. For a long time I contemplated taking my life; ending my pain and the shame of what I'd inflicted on everyone. Finally I realised I had the two best friends in the world: my parents.

That afternoon I sat on the bed with Mum and told her everything. For a long time she said nothing and just cuddled me and stroked my hair. Dad came up and sat on the bed with us and we just talked. Several times Dad threatened to beat the shit out of all of them and Mum had to calm him down. Not once did they blame me. When I tried to put the blame on myself, Mum stopped me.

"You're sixteen and all those fucking bastards are at least ten years older than you, and they're married. They had no right to get involved with you. They should all be going to prison."

It took some effort to convince my parents that confronting them wasn't how I wanted to deal with it. I begged them to let me handle it my own way. I couldn't bear the thought of anything else resulting out of the chaos.

71

Knowing my parents had my back was enough to ignite a spark of courage and level thinking.

I took a few days off work during which time my parents did everything to cheer me up. For the first time I grieved for having let my childhood slip away. Mum was incredible in her support of me, only ever getting cross when I tried to berate myself. It was during that time she shared something about her life which explained her empathy.

"I was unhappy in my first marriage. Len was away a lot and I was left home to look after Robin and Kathleen. A friend of mine lived across the road and we often took the kids out together. She would babysit for me while I slipped down the pub to have a drink.

"That's where I met your Dad. He was working behind the bar and he used to keep an eye on me. Men often tried to chat me up and Dad would come over and send them on their way. I'd stay until closing time and then he'd walk me home."

She laughed with a memory. "One night, I got really drunk and Dad had to piggy-back me. When Len was away Wally would take me and the kids out. Robin adored him because he wasn't rigid and strict like his father. Wally was gentle and funny and kind. When our affair was exposed and out in the open, we also suffered a lot of heartbreak. It wasn't a good time, but we were much older than you. You shouldn't be going through this at your age."

As she told me the rest of the story it dawned on me how much tragedy had impacted their lives. Mum still carried a lot of guilt from that time, but she had no regret for her choices. After listening to her, I was ready to deal with my own problems.

A few days later I went back to work. The first time Luke made a snide comment I glared at him.

"You don't fucking talk to me like that. You don't utter a word to me if you know what's good for you. If you're going to sack me, do it or fuck up."

He stayed away from me, but it wasn't long before the next verbal attack came. Steve's wife was doing a shift at work, something I'm sure Luke set up to needle me. For most of the night I did my job and ignored her constantly berating me with a little help from her friends. I was still repentant enough to take whatever was thrown at me. No one held back and eventually Steve told her to shut her trap.

"Don't get your knickers in a knot," she retorted. "It might cut off your circulation."

Steve sneered. "Well that shouldn't bother you any."

"It doesn't, but I'd hate to have your slut miss out, though she's probably fucking every other guy in here anyway. You don't really think you're the only one, do you?"

I was getting sick of it. The only one paying for our infidelity was me. Luke, Steve and Anne had walked away unscathed. It was even suggested that I had seduced Steve. Unfortunately Kay was in my sights when my temper finally erupted.

She had barely finished her comment when I leaned across the counter, seized her shirt and dragged her over the top, pinning her by the throat.

"Just shut up, just fucking shut up."

A lot of angry people were on me in a second. I was pulled away from her and verbally attacked on all fronts. Luke orchestrated a dramatic finale by picking me up and throwing me out of the building.

"You're fired," he yelled, "Don't ever come back."

I walked away, but I wasn't as upset as I had been. I knew it was finally over. As I headed home some of the guys I knew came after me. It was the first time I knew that not everyone blamed me.

"We knew what was happening. We just didn't want to say anything and get kicked out. We felt sorry for you. Luke, Steve... they're just arseholes. Luke's full of himself. Fuck we laughed when you hammered Kay. She's a right fucking bitch and why should you get all the blame? Anne was screwing Steve as well but she's not owning up to it."

I've never forgotten those boys, George, Jimmy, Adrian, Tim, Rocky and two others both named Mark. They encouraged me to go to Jimmy's house with them. It was just what I needed. We drank, smoked a lot of dope, listened to music and laughed a lot. Not one of them hit on me and they walked me home later. I finally knew there were awesome guys in the world, the kind who respected women and knew how to be good friends without insisting on extras.

I learned a lot that year, and was finally content to lead a quieter life. Diane and I got together more often and she was with me when I had to visit the Family Planning Centre and find out I was five months pregnant.

The only photo of Michael and me together (1979)

CHAPTER TEN

MOTHERS AND BABIES

Those 'good old days' may have had simpler living, but people were no better behaved than they are now. It's just the rules were stricter and the judgements were harsher. People were better at hiding their mistakes. The difference between now and then is that we're not striving to live up to impossible religious principles.

We finally worked out that we're human. There is more acceptance towards marital status, sexuality, children born out of wedlock and anything else which was once deemed 'sinful.' Of course we still have a long way to go.

Mum and Dad were the heroes who challenged the hypocrisy of that rigid, pious society. Their attitudes were at least fifty years ahead of their time.

I have a fond memory of sitting down to watch a movie with my parents in the early seventies. It was the 'Christine Jorgensen Story' and was about the publicised life of a transgender and their subsequent gender reassignment. After a few drinks Dad was always passionate and a bit of a crier over certain movies. He shed a lot of tears during that one.

"Why can't they just accept he doesn't want to be a boy?" he rallied angrily against the television.

Having worked behind a bar most of his life, Dad welcomed and chatted with anyone regardless of status, race or sexuality. He listened to their stories, empathised with their problems and counselled them with his infinite wisdom.

My parents had known and experienced the cruelty inflicted on anyone who didn't live a 'normal' or 'godly' life. They were rebels and I love them for it.

They faced the situation of their pregnant sixteen year-old daughter like everything else they had come up against; with calmness, simplicity, acceptance and a little humour. I remember well the day I shared my news with Mum.

I was sitting on her bed, watching her do her make-up and hair. She glanced at my reflection a few times grinning but saying nothing. Finally I found the nerve to speak up.

"Mum, I've got something to tell you."

She laughed. "Did you think I didn't know?"

My mouth fell open. "How...?"

"I'm your mother. Just tell me what you've decided to do about this."

"I want my baby."

"Good. So we better start getting things ready."

"How do you think Dad will feel about it?"

"Your father?" Mum laughed. "How do you think he's going to feel? The same way I do. A baby is coming into our lives. What's there not to be happy about?"

And that was it. No dramas, no tears or anything negative. Mum and Dad were thrilled to be having another baby in their lives. There was no lectures on how hard it would be for me, or how it would change my life. Instead they had full confidence in my ability to be a mother at seventeen. There was certainly no hiding it. They proudly told everyone they were going to be grandparents. Anyone who suggested anything negative was quickly shut down.

It was a wonderful time of my life and I was allowed and encouraged to enjoy the anticipation of becoming a mother. I read countless books about childbirth and parenting. Mum and I knitted clothes and painted furniture for a nursery. There was a constant atmosphere of anticipation and excitement.

The day I went into labour was a little odd. There were a few minor contractions, but mostly it was the nausea I felt which prompted me to go to hospital. I fully expected to come home again, even though the baby was six days overdue.

At the hospital I waited patiently until a nurse came to see me and then only complained about having a bad stomach ache. It was when she examined me that a little panic set in.

"My dear girl, you're in advanced labour. Your cervix is nearly fully dilated. We need to get you into the labour ward now."

By then it was nearly five o'clock and I'd only been ill for a couple of hours. From what I'd read in the books, I was going to be in labour for hours. Once they had me in the labour ward I was immediately given gas, but I didn't like the feeling doped up. I'd looked forward to this moment and wanted to experience everything. I had been reading books about breathing techniques to control pain and told the attending staff I wanted to do things my own way.

All that got me was knowing grins and condescending remarks. "We'll see."

It was the doctor who finally believed in me, just over an hour later. "Storm, you're doing incredibly well. You just keep listening to what I tell you and you're going to be holding your baby soon."

The contractions were brutal, but they didn't frighten me. I listened and followed every direction the doctor gave me, breathing and panting through the pain and pushing on each contraction. An hour later my son was born and placed in my arms as promised. A few minutes later, I was breastfeeding him, while continually bawling with happiness.

Later, the doctor came to see us in the ward. I was calm, relaxed and feeding my son without any problems. He had come to tell me how impressed he had been with me.

"You had no pain relief and you were so calm, and you followed my instructions to the point I didn't need to do an episiotomy. For a first timer and such a young mum, birthing an eight-pound baby..." He shook his head and laughed. "These breathing techniques you mentioned?"

I nodded. "I read loads of books about them. It seemed the way to go for me."

"I'm going to have to do some reading up on it myself." He smiled.

Whether it was the breathing or something entirely different, through four childbirths and all of them big babies, I was never in labour longer than four hours, never had pain relief or needed stitches. My third child arrived within half an hour of getting to hospital. By my fourth child, I just stayed at home and had him there, with two midwives and my husband, children and Mum all in the room with me.

Mum was constantly crying and disappearing. I went out to find her.

"What's wrong Mum?"

"You're in so much pain," she sobbed.

I laughed. "Good pain, Mum, nothing I'm afraid of."

"I've never experienced this," she told me. "When I had Robin and Kathleen, I was put to sleep and woke up to them waiting for me."

"Then, please Mum, please come and enjoy this with me. It's incredible. What do you reckon Mum, a boy or a girl?"

"Oh, definitely a boy."

"Then come and see your grandson being born. There is nothing more beautiful in the world than seeing a baby come into it."

She was right about a boy of course, and when Daniel was born, she was the first to cradle him in her arms. Sharing that with her was one of the most precious moments of my life, as was being with my daughters throughout their labours.

Despite my age I handled motherhood well from the outset. I loved being a mother and being involved in my son's life, made easier with Mum and Dad's support. There were always prejudices around me towards single mothers, especially ones as young as me, but I ignored it just as Mum and Dad had ignored everything which society had wanted to enforce upon them.

The principles they taught me were priceless, the best of them about believing in myself and having confidence in my decisions. Just as important was equipping myself to make those decisions by getting educated, listening and being open-minded. These are the same principles I have strived to pass on to my children.

Thankfully their lives haven't been as dysfunctional as mine, but I constantly see in them the legacy Mum and Dad left behind. They're confident and believe in themselves. I see it in their lives, their chosen careers and in their role as parents. They're outspoken about bigotry and passionate about educating themselves.

My husband and I are Christians, and we chose to send them to Christian schools, but our children were encouraged to question everything and find their own beliefs. They chose to be atheist and we're fine with that. It makes some lively family discussions around the Sunday family dinner table.

They are huge fans of Terry Pratchett books and I once said to my daughter, "You know you wouldn't fully appreciate his humour if you didn't know the bible."

My daughter laughed. "Wow, Mum, you are so right."

While I don't spout Bible passages often, there is one which has always resonated with me, for the way you can swap the word 'love' for 'a parent.'

A parent is patient and kind. A parent doesn't envy or boast or dishonour others. Parents are not self-seeking or easily angered. They keep no records of wrongs. Parents don't delight in evil, but rejoice with the truth. Parents always protect, always trust, always hope and always persevere.

The word 'always' speaks of perfection. Maybe 'strive to' should be thrown in there somewhere. We don't always get it right, but accepting our shortcomings is just as necessary.

There's another lesson in this chapter about reading a lot of books. Thanks Dad.

Michael, Julie and Clinton

79

CHAPTER ELEVEN

THE EIGHTIES

Before Clinton's first birthday Julie and Michael had separated. He had cheated on her too many times, but I was still hopeful they would eventually get back together. It was with Julie and Clinton I saw Michael's only chance of finding happiness.

I admired Julie for her tenacity and determination to put Clinton's welfare first. She worked long hours, kept a lovely home and kept Michael's criminal activities far away from him. Through the years we shared a hope of seeing Michael find peace. It was humbling knowing Julie still loved him after everything he'd put her through.

On a beautiful day in October we sat on the lawn and celebrated Clinton's first birthday. It was the first of many he would never get to share with his dad. For the next few years the same pattern continued for me; writing letters and visiting Michael in prison. At some point after his release he was living down south with a new girlfriend. I visited once but the long journey on buses and trains was too daunting.

For a long time I didn't hear from him. Just after my son's second birthday Michael turned up and asked if he could stay with me. I was living in the house next door to Mum and Dad, having taken it over from Gladys and Pete.

For years we'd spent such little time together and it was wonderful having him back in my life. He was a fun uncle and would sit down with my son, helping him with a Lego construction. It brought back so many memories of our childhood together.

For a few months it was like those very early days when our family was together and happy. We still got visits from Robin with the wonderful addition of a wife and children. We loved Rose and their beautiful children, Aaron and Blaise.

From the outset Robin had told Rose that I was his daughter and explained our weird family history. I no longer thought about it. As far I was concerned we were family, despite our oddities. To me, Robin was still my brother and Aaron and Blaise were my nephew and niece.

It wasn't long before Michael was restless again. Like Julie, I had firm rules about keeping his criminal life away from us. For the most part he complied, but there were times when it came close to home.

Nothing annoyed me more than hearing the deep thrum of a Harley Davidson idling outside my house. Michael was a patched member of the *Comancheros* motorcycle gang, just one of the many biker associations he'd been with over the years. Their unwelcomed visit usually heralded Michael's return to a criminal life.

Many of them had abusive histories similar to Michael's. Some of them were Vietnam veterans who had been discarded by society. I understood his need for them, but despaired that he couldn't find peace within the family who loved him and were ready to be there for him; who would constantly forgive his crimes and ignore Michael's inclination towards thieving.

Mum and Dad's pension cheques began to disappear on the day they were due. I took Mum to Social Security, only to discover they'd been cashed. As usual, my parents were quick to dismiss Michael as the culprit, but we all knew it was him. Replacing them meant getting the police involved, but Mum and Dad refused to do that. They chose to go without their income rather than have him locked up again. It made me angry.

Once Michael came for a walk with me and my son as I went to collect mail from my previous rented abode. No one was home, but the blinds were up and we could see into the bedroom. There was a clock radio on the bedside cabinet and a distinctively patterned quilt on the bed. The next day they were in Michael's bedroom, along with many other items. It was the only time I ever got furious with him.

"Why would you do that? Why do you have this constant need to steal things? And how could you do that to me? Do you think I want to go through all that again, police turning up at the door and going through my house? And while we at it, leave Mum and Dad's pension alone. It's all they have to live on."

My words cut through him and I could see he was hurt. I was his loyal, loving sister, the one person who had never given up on him, who had always visited and written letters whenever he was locked up. At that moment I was just weary of all his bullshit and frustrated by his determination to sabotage his life.

Soon after he moved out, and within a short time was back in jail. As soon as I knew I resumed my visits. One day, upon arrival to Yatala Prison, I was thrilled to see Julie and Clinton were visiting as well.

I realised I wasn't the only one who had refused to give up on him. Julie had suffered much more than I had; dealing with his behaviour, catching him out with other women and through all that, raising their son alone. I know Michael loved Clinton. For those times he was there as a dad he was loving and attentive, but those times were too short and too far apart. Julie was always left to deal with the hurt and disappointment Michael caused them every time he walked away.

Life went on. My days were filled with the enjoyment of being a mum. I took my son everywhere - to playgroup, the toy library and the playground. With Mum and Dad next door I had plenty of support and two very willing babysitters. The constant doting and spoiling I had received as a child was doubled for Lee.

We had acquired a new member in our family, a German Shephard named Coruba. Like Herman, she had a sweet temperament and wasn't hostile to anyone, but could be fiercely protective of Lee. She was wary of strangers being too close to him and would watch every move and growl quietly. It was comforting having her around. At night all three of us would end up in my bed.

I stayed close to home, reluctant to engage a social life. Some self-reflection over past behaviour had calmed me right down. I was content to have coffee with friends and do some babysitting for them.

It was on one of these occasions I experienced another terrifying encounter with a male. My friend Barbara had three boys who were all good friends with Lee. One night I took Lee and went to her place to watch the children while Barbara and her husband went out.

Barbara often did short-term foster care and I was used to seeing teenagers staying with her. On this particular night the children weren't long in bed when I heard the back door open. I was halfway down the hall when I saw two teenage boys enter, one of whom was carrying a rifle.

My insides withered as he looked at me and raised the muzzle in my direction.

"Where's Barbara?" he demanded.

Somehow I managed to stay calm and smiled. "She's out tonight, but if you need anything I can help out."

His friend was panicking. "Eddie, man, don't be doing this shit. Let's just go."

I was nodding furiously inside. *Please, please, go.*

"No. I need to think," Eddie said, pacing about, glancing at me and keeping the rifle pointed in my direction.

"How about a coffee and a ciggy?" I suggested. "That always helps me think."

Eddie seemed to like the idea but kept the rifle trained on me as I forced myself into the kitchen. I was trembling as I filled the kettle and set out the cups.

"My smokes are in my bag there on the table," I said. "Help yourself."

The gun was laid down as Eddie got out my smokes. He lit one, but I wasn't going to be the one to suggest there was no smoking in the house.

"Light me one too," I said as I brought their coffees and sat down with them.

I could see the dilated pupils of Eddie's eyes and knew he was high on something. My only thought was the four little boys asleep in their bedroom and I prayed desperately none of them would wake up.

Eddie's friend grew more agitated and I feared him escalating the situation. I kept supplying cigarettes and talked about anything which came to mind. When they were relaxed enough I casually related their options.

"One way or another, we're eventually going to have police on our doorstep. If they see that rifle it's all going to go to hell, you know that don't you? Right now, nothing's happened. Why don't we keep it that way? Fuck off and leave the rifle with me."

"Yeah," Eddie scoffed. "And you'll just tell Barbara anyway and the cops will be after me."

"You're fucking right I'm going to tell her, but you'll be long gone before she finds out, hopefully somewhere where you can straighten up and don't have a fucking firearm. When the police do catch up with you, all you'll get is a slap on the wrist. So wise up and just leave so I can enjoy the rest of my night."

His friend was nodding. "Yeah Eddie, she's right and I don't want any fucking trouble over guns. Can we go?"

Whatever time passed I couldn't say. My most vivid recall was the moment they left the house. I finally succumbed to the fear which had been suppressed until then, sinking to the floor and thanking whatever God or universal force had saved our lives that night, kept the children in bed and me from panicking. At that time I was still very much agnostic.

When Barbara and her husband arrived home I was calm again. The police were called and questioned me about Eddie's visit. For some reason I chose to downplay how bad it had been, though I certainly mentioned he'd had a rifle with him.

It was well after midnight before Lee and I were driven home. As I lay in bed I recalled every terrifying minute but felt satisfied over my handling of the situation. It had me contemplating the possibility of some sort of career in social work. I had a knack for talking with people and keeping a cool head in volatile situations.

It seems I wasn't the only one who thought about that night. In my early days of dating my husband, Eddie showed up at my front door though I don't know how he'd found out where I lived. He was straight and asked rather sheepishly if he could talk to me. I invited him in and introduced him to Andrew as a 'friend of mine.'

Eddie had reflected on what he had done that night and realised how much worse it could have been. He stayed for an hour during which time he gave me a rather 'beat-around-the-bush' apology and even joked about some of it. He told me he had listened to me and had left the rifle in Barbara's laundry. By the time the police had caught up with him he was clearheaded and co-operative.

"You were right," he said. "I got a slap on the wrist and put away for a few months."

In the end I gave him what he had come for - forgiveness.

After he left Andrew frowned and peered at me. "Well that was weird. What the hell was he talking about?"

I grinned. "That was Eddie. He held me at gunpoint one night while I was babysitting."

Andrew was shocked and raised the possibility of discouraging any further visits from Eddie. That was a given, and we never did get another visit. I'd like to think Eddie went on to do something good with his life. I think I saw in Eddie the chance of pulling himself out of a life on a downward spiral. My years with Michael had given me an empathy for youth who had lost their way or were venting their rage against the circumstances of their lives. Society's solution was to put them in a punitive system under the guise of rehabilitation. I can't help thinking some tenderness and a few random acts of kindness would do more good.

Some years later I did venture into social work and saw the flaws and prejudices within the system. I once sat with a man who had just told me about the circumstances leading up to his descent into alcoholism.

One day he was living a happy normal life, the same as anyone in a good middle-class family environment. With one devastating accident everything changed for him and his family.

I cried and wiped away tears as he related his story. He stopped and stared at me.

"I've told this story to loads of counsellors and shrinks, but I've never seen anyone cry before."

"Yeah, I'm pretty bad as this, sorry." I grinned. "I'm a real sook and I get a bit too invested."

He shook his head. "No, don't apologise. I'm stunned. For the first time in years I feel as if someone is actually listening."

I was listening, but his story had made me realise something else: None of us are immune from that one incident which might rip us out of our comfortable lives and change everything. It could have been my experience with Eddie, but it wasn't.

Throughout my first twenty years I learned quite a bit about life: about people, about being a mum and having empathy for others. Michael was an essential part of my education about broken lives, and how sometimes we just can't fix them. All we can do is be there for them and show them someone cares.

CHAPTER TWELVE

LOVE AND OTHER MUSES

Andrew

After Lee's third birthday I began dating again, but little had changed about my opinion of men. A first date was rarely followed up by another. I had Lee to think about and I wasn't about to bring some arsehole into our lives. I began to believe I would be single for life and it was a little depressing.

Diane and I were seeing more of each other, though it required two bus rides to visit her. One day when I was there her husband came home with his friend, Andrew, a tall, dark and attractive guy who had a brilliant sense of humour. His witty replies had me in tears with laughter. When I got set to leave, Diane jumped in and told Andrew to drive me home.

He was fairly eager to comply, but on the way home his car broke down. I could see he was embarrassed as he got out to push it to the side of the road. I got out to help him, but he became flustered.

"No way. You just sit in the car. I can push it on my own."

I did as I was told, simply because I could see how embarrassed he was. After tinkering with the engine he got the car started again and got me home, where he jumped out and ran around to open the door for me.

I expected him to linger, but he simply smiled and bade me goodbye. I was a little disappointed as he drove off. When I saw Diane next, she told me that Andrew had really liked me and thought I was beautiful, but she'd warned him off of me.

"You don't want to go there. Storm is a wild one and chews men up and spits them out."

I laughed, knowing she wasn't wrong and I could see she was a little protective of Andrew.

"He's a really nice guy, a proper gentleman."

I took no offence at her concern knowing how well she knew my history. I had dated a couple of friends of her family and left a little heartbreak behind, which hadn't gone down well with her sisters. For her sake I didn't pursue anything more about Andrew, but he had other ideas.

A few weeks later there was a knock at my front door. I opened it to see an intoxicated man wearing dark sunglasses and leaning on the wall to keep upright. He was tattooed and wearing a dark blue singlet and cut-off jean shorts. Out on the street, another man with tattoos and a big, bushy beard was waiting for him in a car.

"Hi," I frowned. "Can I help you?"

He slurred an answer. "I was wondering if you wanted to go to a party with me on Saturday afternoon."

I laughed. "Sure, and who are you?"

He lifted his sunglasses and I could see he was a little hurt by my ignorance. "I'm Andrew. We met at Diane's place."

"Oh, Andrew. Yes, I do remember you, and sure, I'll go. Who's your mate?"

"That's Rob. I live with him and his girlfriend, and two other couples. We're having a housewarming party."

"Sounds like fun. I'll look forward to seeing you on Saturday."

He seemed thrilled with my answer and mumbled something about picking me up and a nervous goodbye before stumbling back to the car. I laughed and couldn't help thinking how good-looking he was, even when he was drunk. I was intrigued at the prospect of spending time with him.

Saturday arrived and, as usual, I devoted time to my make-up and picking the right outfit. I was strangely excited about Andrew's arrival but still cautious. A friend had asked me to babysit that night and I'd accepted.

Having to come home to babysit was always a good excuse if a date wasn't working out.

At 2.30pm Andrew arrived, sober and wearing a black t-shirt and jeans. I was startled by my instant attraction to his lean, muscled body and tattooed biceps, but I wasn't as open about it as he was. He plainly stared at me, wide-eyed.

"Wow, you look really beautiful."

He was something completely different, without any false bravado. He was clearly nervous, but we talked and laughed all the way to the party. When we arrived he pulled up and grinned at me.

"Do you smoke dope?"

"I do," I smiled.

He pulled out a tin and started to pack a pipe, but was shaking so much he kept dropping the weed. Getting stoned helped relax him and we entered the backyard where the party was happening. His flatmates and friends were quick to greet me, some of them giving him a hearty slap on the back. I learned later they had encouraged him to ask me out.

For the next few hours, over a few drinks, we laughed and talked and had the best time together. I was stunned to learn of his love of reading and his views on social issues. His friends were making enough remarks for me to understand how alike we were in something else. Andrew had been with a lot of girls and didn't do relationships either.

When I had to get home, he drove me there and told me how much he'd enjoyed the afternoon. Then he was back in the car to return to the party. A little of me was regretting having made plans to babysit, but it was too late to cancel.

I thought about Andrew long into the night, which was something new for me. It didn't bother me that he was only one year older, because there was a maturity about him I respected. I couldn't stop thinking about him and wanting to see him again. I got my wish.

The next day Andrew showed up at lunchtime and met Lee. Immediately, I could see he was good with kids and Lee seemed to like him. My parents were a bit more dubious about this tattooed young man with his singlet and threadbare jeans.

Andrew took me back to his place where they were still cleaning up from the party. Everyone seemed surprised and a little nervous to see me. I soon found out why when an attractive blonde called by to see Andrew.

He tried to meet her before she got too close to me, but I had already guessed they had hooked up. It didn't bother me and I told him so after she had gone. His mate, Rob, felt relaxed enough to then relate the sordid details.

Instead of upsetting me, I was intrigued. From what I was hearing, Andrew was quite adventurous when it came to sex. Still, he didn't want me getting put off and got me out of there fast. We spent the rest of the day together laughing, talking and having fun. Not once did he make any moves on me. At the end of the day he brought me home and bid me goodnight.

I had a long restless night, unable to get him out of my thoughts. He was so different from any other guy I had dated and I couldn't understand why he hadn't even tried to kiss me. On Monday he turned up again and once again all we did was talk. It was as he was leaving I could see he was worried about something.

He grinned. "Would it be alright to kiss you goodnight?"

I nearly laughed, but then politely gave him permission. The kiss was sweet and lingering, but after our lips had parted he was gone. Andrew told me later that he was so worked-up over it he drove off the wrong way and somehow ended up in the Adelaide Hills. He wasn't the only one who was feeling the giddiness of love.

Tuesday came and Andrew was back. We lay on the couch together, talking and watching Monty Python, something else we had in common, but neither of us was concentrating on the television. At one stage I stared into his dark, brown eyes and finally allowed myself to acknowledge what I was feeling. I was in love and knew at that moment I wanted to spend the rest of my life with this man.

I got off the couch and went to my bedroom where I went through my rather impressive collection of lingerie. I picked a long, black, silky gown and changed into it. When I returned to the living room, his mouth dropped open.

"I'm going to bed," I told him. "You're welcome to join me."

Sure enough, he followed and went to switch the light out.

"No, leave it on," I told him. "I want to see you."

Andrew and I often laugh about that night. He continues to maintain he was a helpless, green lad, swept up and seduced by a siren who had a lot of weird demands, all which he met. In fact, he had no qualms about me taking the lead. The next morning I told him to marry me. Andrew still tells everyone that he just did what he was told.

He certainly didn't run. Five days after our first date Andrew moved in with me, much to Coruba's disapproval at having to give up my bed. Lee hadn't made up his mind about it. Seeing how close they are these days, it's easy to forget there were many years and several rocky paths to navigate before Lee finally accepted Andrew.

A week later, when Andrew and I announced our engagement, everyone was stunned. No one could believe it. My friends thought I had lost my mind, but I'd never been so certain about anything in my life.

"I'm in love," I told them. "For the first time in my life, I'm in love."

I'm sure there were bets on how long we'd last, but we easily beat the odds. Thirty-six years, four children and six grandchildren later, we're more in love than ever. The years have blended our souls together, and the memories of those first days together are cherished. I had found the love of my life and my days of loneliness were over.

Soon after our engagement I took Andrew to Yatala Prison to meet Michael. They got on well, but then Michael started talking about smuggling marijuana in on our next visit. Andrew didn't seem opposed to the idea, but as we headed home I made my position quite clear.

"That's not happening. I love my brother and I'll always support him, but I won't allow his crimes anywhere near my life."

Andrew was fine with that. He didn't like the idea either but had wanted Michael to like him. One of the oddest visits we made was to the low-security prison. We got to sit on a lawn in the sunshine where other families were visiting inmates. Bottles of alcohol-tainted coke were passed around and the air was rife with marijuana.

Andrew was stunned but nothing surprised me about these prisons. Through the years of visiting every institution in the state I saw some strange sights, from drugs being passed openly to inmates, to a couple engaged in sex. In some places the rules were blatantly relaxed and in others, like Adelaide Gaol, the security was daunting. A couple of my visits were conducted through a thick pane of glass and with the use of phones to talk to one another. I longed for a day where I would never have to see another prison again and then regretted it years later.

It was wonderful having Andrew with me to visit Michael and not just because of the convenient transport. I had someone who empathised with my despair of walking away after every visit, feeling as if I was abandoning Michael. With Michael due for release in August we set a date for our wedding.

Yet again, I was faced with disappointment. While at Cadell, Michael had been implicated in the burning down of a shed. He seemed to think nothing would come of it but his release was put back until January. My anticipation and hope of a joyous and rare family celebration was bitterly deflated.

As it turned out, Michael's extended sentence proved to be a blessing. Being a member of the *Comancheros* motorcycle gang and, in all likelihood, he would have been present at one of Australia's most notorious events, the Milperra Massacre.

On Father's Day, the 2nd September 1984, gang members from the *Comancheros* and *Bandidos* went up against each other in the carpark of the Viking Tavern in Milperra, a suburb of Sydney. Their brutal attacks on each other involved high-powered rifles, lead pipes and chains. At the end of it seven people were dead, including an innocent 15 year-old girl.

For the first time ever, I was grateful for Michael's incarceration and could forgive his absence from our wedding. In the weeks which followed, Andrew and I made our simple preparations and they really were simple.

We shopped for my wedding dress together at a Salvation Army Op Shop. The price on the one we both loved was ten dollars, but they were having a half-price sale that day. We still laugh about that.

On the 24th November 1984, Andrew and I were married at a simple ceremony at the Registry Office. There were no trimmings, just a few friends present and even fewer family members to celebrate with us. Robin's wife was due to have another baby, so driving 1,200 kilometres from Canberra was impossible. Andrew's family was in New Zealand, but none of them made the journey.

Only his brother living in South Australia came along with his wife. I think there was still an idea Andrew and I wouldn't last. My family was just

Mum, Dad, Lee and Susan, who was my bridesmaid. As for friends, the dearest of them were there for me, Diane, Gladys, Pete and Mrs Best.

Despite those who couldn't or didn't want to be there, our wedding day was glorious. My parents lamented not having the funds to provide me with something fancier, but my needs were simple. Mum got to see me walk down a small aisle on the arm of my very proud father. Diane was at my side as my Matron-of-Honour. Mum and Dad both had the joy of knowing I was marrying the man I loved; a man not so much different from Dad in his commitment to me; a man who would always cherish, honour and strive to make me happy to our last days.

The reception was a quiet affair in which Andrew and I cooked and served up the food ourselves. Neither of us drank much, and at the end we drove all the inebriated people home, including my parents. Our wedding night was spent in our own bed and there was no honeymoon, but I was as happy as any bride could possibly be. I was also three months pregnant with our eldest daughter.

Me and Dad on my wedding day

24th November 1984

A beautiful day in my $5 wedding dress with the man of my dreams

CHAPTER THIRTEEN

FINAL DAYS

Early in the New Year of 1985 Michael got out of prison and came to stay with us. Again, I had hopes his life would turn about, especially when he reunited with Julie soon after. By then, Clinton was eight years-old and such a lovely boy. He looked just like his father, with Michael's dark skin and black hair. Only his beautiful blue-green eyes were different from the brown and amber eyes of his parents.

My hopes were further encouraged when Julie announced she was having another baby. It had taken some convincing when Michael had begged her to have another child with him. Julie had already worked hard and without support to make certain Clinton's life was happy and secure.

Another baby was going to be a challenge, but Julie was as hopeful as I was. Through all the heartbreak, infidelity, the times in prison and being left alone to raise their son, Julie continued to love Michael.

Mother's Day was approaching and it seemed a good time to celebrate our growing family. It was decided that we would have a family picnic in the South Parklands, where Michael and I had spent so much time with Dad in our early years. The dogs could run around and Lee and Clinton had the playground to entertain them. Mum did some baking and Julie came over to help me prepare the food, telling me Michael would meet us there. Andrew made sure he had some beers for Dad.

It was a chilly day with rain threatening, but nothing could dampen my excitement. I had my camera packed, determined to capture every special moment and the family pictures we lacked. Photos from our childhood were scarce. There were none of Michael and me together or even any with our parents. I planned to change that.

We arrived at the park and the day got underway. We were having a wonderful time, but Michael still hadn't shown up. Lunch was served and there was still no sign of him. I was angry he had spoiled this moment and disappointed for Mum. There had been too many Mother's Days without her son and I know she had looked forward to this one. It was such a lovely time and photos were taken but Michael was in none of them.

In the late afternoon we said goodbye to Julie and Clinton. Julie promised to give Michael a good telling-off when she got home but he wasn't there. Instead, a note was left for her:

"Julie, I'm in trouble. I have to go but I'll be back before the baby is born. I love you."

Neither Julie nor I were overly worried. Michael disappearing was something with which we were familiar. There was no doubting we would eventually get a visit from the police, or a letter from Michael or he would just turn up on the doorstep. Whether it was months or a couple of years, he always came back.

Julie had to face the prospect of raising another baby alone and Clinton was again without the Dad he adored. At least, this time she knew she had us, her family, to turn to. She was furious and determined to keep Michael out of her life, but she never quite got him out of her heart. When months turned into years without any sign of Michael, we began to fear the worst.

We decided to file a 'missing person' report. The police investigated and soon after, a police officer called us back in. They had one mug shot of Michael and a sighting of him in Kings Cross in Sydney from a few years earlier. The officer was blunt.

"There's been no record of him being in any prison during that time, or any crime reports on Michael. Let's face it, he's a bad character and if he hasn't had some kind of brush with the law in all that time, then we can only conclude that he's dead."

There was no sympathy, just a cold brutal answer which we had somewhat suspected. We were shattered at having to accept the conclusion. The file would remain open until they knew for certain, at which time they would inform us, but we shouldn't get our hopes up. We both grieved deeply for him. Julie was faced with having to tell her boys. For years I often had dark thoughts of Michael having died violently and been left lying in a shallow grave somewhere.

For years Julie refused to move, always hopeful of a knock on the door and seeing Michael's guilty, grinning face looking back at her. We remained a close family and were together at Christmas until our move to New Zealand in 2001. Julie still tells me off for moving so far away from her.

95

Mother's Day became a reminder of Michael's disappearance. I've looked at the photos I took that day and reflected on what we might have done differently. Michael should have been in all of them and his absence haunted me through the years.

The police never got back to us. Julie and I longed for closure and finally, and reluctantly, accepted we would never know what had become of Michael. The brother I loved was gone forever.

Mother's Day 1985

CHAPTER FOURTEEN

The GOING DOWN OF THE SUN

On a cold, bleak night in May 1988, I was playing competition 8-ball at a city pub when I was summoned to the phone. It was a friend of ours, informing me that Andrew was headed to my parents' house. Dad had collapsed and was being taken to hospital in an ambulance. I quietly asked a team member if she could drive me to their house.

On the way we passed the ambulance. I remained calm until I was suddenly struck with a bizarre notion, a strange absolute certainty which made me panic and gasp desperately. My friend asked if I was alright.

I slowly settled down and nodded. "My Dad has died."

She looked at me, startled. "No, Storm, no. He's going to be alright. Don't think the worse. He's going to be fine."

"Yeah, you're right," I replied, but the grim certainty remained.

Right then I began mentally preparing myself to be available for Mum. My heart was already breaking for her, unable to comprehend her life without Dad. For nearly forty years they had been inseparable, so much more than just husband and wife. They were best friends, lovers, soul-mates. They were everything to each other.

When we arrived at their house Andrew rushed to greet me, distraught and trying hard to keep calm. I reassured him and went to Mum who was standing with the neighbours, looking confused.

"I don't know what happened, Storm. Dad had just cooked our dinner and we were eating when he said he had some indigestion and might have a lie down on the bed. I went up to see him, and he was sweating and breathing funny. I got a flannel and wiped his face for him and held his hand, but I got scared when he wouldn't wake up. I thought I'd better get some help."

The landlord's son was living in the attached house next door. He had gone back with her and in less than a minute was rushing back to his place to call an ambulance. Mum and Dad had never possessed a phone.

Andrew got us into the car and took us to hospital, where we were led to a room on our own. Eventually a doctor and nurse came to see us.

"I'm so very sorry," the doctor said. "Mr Taylor suffered a coronary and was unable to be revived. He passed away in the ambulance."

Whatever was said after that went unheard. Andrew crumpled in tears and sank back into the chair. I immediately pulled Mum into my arms and held her as tightly as I could. Her sobs ripped through me as I stood holding her.

When Andrew came to comfort me I shook my head. "I'm alright. We need to get Mum back to our place and into bed. I want to make sure Dad's things will be bagged up properly, and there's probably something to sign."

I looked at the nurse who stayed with us. "Can we see him?"

"Of course."

Dad was laid out on a hospital bed with a sheet pulled up to his bare shoulders, his skin looking sallow and shiny. Mum sobbed as she leaned on him, kissing him repeatedly and stroking his head.

"He's so cold."

She looked so much older and frail, her petite form trembling with grief and fear. For a moment I feared losing both of them.

"We need to get you home to bed, Mum," I told her. "You need rest and warmth or your arthritis will be flaring out of control again. I'll make sure Dad is looked after, I promise."

I looked at Andrew, his eyes swollen and red from crying. "Start taking Mum to the car and hold on to her so her legs don't give out on her. I'll be along soon."

He nodded and did as I asked. When they had gone from the room, I kissed Dad and held his hand. "I'll look after her, Dad. I promise. Don't take her with you now. I need her, too."

When I caught up with them, Andrew was carrying Mum in his arms, and together we got her into the car. He looked at me with concern.

"I'm alright," I assured him. "Let's just look after Mum."

We drove to Mum's house and picked up Tess, before taking them back to our place. We broke the news to our friends who were looking after our children. Thankfully the kids were fast asleep, oblivious to having lost their beloved Pa. As we said goodbye to our friends, the police pulled up in our driveway.

Andrew went to speak to them and returned to me looking worried. "They want to ask your Mum some questions."

"Yeah, well that's not happening." I went out to see them myself.

One officer started talking about the time it had taken for Mum to get help and I cut him off angrily.

"Because she didn't understand what was happening, because she's crippled up with rheumatoid arthritis and for the fact there's no fucking phone in the house. It would have taken her a long time just to walk next door to get help."

"Was there any trouble between...?"

"Don't go there. My parents loved each other. Dad looked after Mum, not the other way round. He did everything for her: the housework, the cooking, the shopping... Mum couldn't do any of that."

"Can we...?"

"No, you can't. Mum has just lost the man she loved. There's nothing sinister behind it. He died, and she hasn't even begun to come to grips with that. Whatever you're thinking is a fucking load of rubbish, as you would find out if you asked anyone who has ever known my parents. Leave us the fuck alone and don't go near my mother."

They left and we never heard anything more from them. My anger at them fuelled my adrenaline to keep a clear head. I got Mum into bed with Tess and a hot water bottle, and made sure she had taken all her pills.

"I'll stay with you, Mum."

She shook her head. "I want to be alone. You go get some rest."

Tess snuggled up against her and lay her head down on her paws. Her sad eyes stared out at nothing, as if deep in thought and silently grieving. From that moment, Tess never left Mum's side and became fiercely protective of her. She died a few years later at the ripe old age of nineteen years, snarling at anyone who got too close. Only our children were exempt from her temper and allowed to sit with Mum on her chair. A few times Andrew and I got a nip, and even our German Shepherd knew better than to annoy her.

Well after midnight I joined Andrew in the kitchen. He looked weary and still in shock, but immediately started to fuss over me.

"I'm alright, love," I insisted.

"You're not alright. You've just lost your dad and you're pregnant. You should go to the spare bed and try and get some sleep."

"I won't sleep. You take the bed and I'll curl up on the couch and watch some TV. You've worked all day and there's a lot to do tomorrow. We have to pack up Mum's house and work out how we're going to fit it all in, and I've got to arrange the funeral. I need time to think."

"You're worrying me." Andrew held me. "You haven't cried at all. That can't be good."

"I don't know why, but I'm sure I'll be a wreck by the morning."

It took a few days before the tears came, and only when I was alone in my parents' empty house. An eerie sanity had prevailed to allow me to get everything done and care for Mum, Andrew and our kids. Their grief was my only concern. As I sat on floor in the bedroom where Dad's life had ebbed away, I shook my head.

"Wow, Dad, did you really have to do this now? You didn't even wait to see this baby born. I'm so pissed off with you. I'm going to have my hands full now; three kids and Mum to care for. You just left us knowing I would do it, didn't you?"

I think those first few days I kept hearing Dad saying to me, "No use bawling about it. What's done is done. Crying about it isn't going to help so just buck up and carry on."

He wasn't going to get away with it that easily. As I sat in that room, the tears finally came and didn't let up for a long time. As I grieved the loss of my Dad, my best friend, I reiterated my promise to look after Mum. There was never any suggestion of putting her in a retirement home. Many years later I spoke about it with Andrew.

"I never even discussed it with you, or wondered what your feelings were about it. I just moved Mum and Tess in with us."

"There was nothing to discuss," Andrew told me. "Your Mum had lost Wally and she needed to be cared for. I knew you weren't about to let anyone else do that, and neither was I. She belonged with us."

Mum lived with us for six years and it was perfect. She just fitted in with us and was able to spoil the kids easier, but helped us out in any way she could. One time Andrew and I had an awful argument, yelling at each other and calling each other names. We can't even remember what it was about, but Andrew started pulling my clothes out of the wardrobe and tossing them out on the front lawn. I was yelling back and calling him every horrible name I could think of.

In the midst of this Mum was quietly shuffling about, picking up my clothes and folding them up into a neat pile. She didn't say a word and just let us go for it. She knew I could look after myself and she wasn't about to side with either of us, having every confidence we would sort it out. We finally noticed what Mum was doing and realised what idiots were being. We've often laughed about that moment and remembered how devastated we were when she wasn't there anymore.

Mum passed away peacefully in her bed with Robin and me beside her. Our family home was never quite the same without her. Somehow we had made it work, and lived happily with three adults, four children and two dogs in a cramped three-bedroomed house. Mum's absence was an enormous hole in our lives.

Dad's death was equally devastating. The Australian Army helped out with most of the funeral and his coffin was draped in the Australian flag. Several of his old Army buddies showed up in uniform and spoke about him. In their reverence of him, they stood silently and saluted Dad's coffin. They wiped tears away, as we all did, when the *Last Post* was played and poppies were laid on the coffin.

There were people who came up to us afterwards to say many good things about Dad. Some introduced themselves as cousins, which intrigued me a little. I knew a lot about Dad's immediate family but little about his other relatives.

A few weeks after Dad's funeral I attended my first meeting of the Genealogy Society of South Australia to learn about researching family history. I finally wanted an insight into my family and the events which had led to my birth, but it was more than that. By researching Dad's family tree, it was as if he was beside me, reminding me of all those anecdotes he'd spoken of.

It took only one meeting to ignite a passion which has spanned thirty years and a family tree of over nine thousand people. I was determined to learn the truth behind the stories I'd been told by my parents and the ones they never knew. Through it all I had hoped to stumble upon the truth about my biological father.

My research had raised doubts of Robin's claim to that role, something I never told him. I was far too humbled by his love and pride in me as his daughter. Until he passed away, I refused to do any tests which would give me certainty one way or the other.

As much as I loved Robin, I only ever had one Dad; the man who had raised me and gave me a love of books, movies and poetry; who had taught me about gentleness, forgiveness and acceptance. He had been the perfect example of how a man should love and honour a woman. He allowed me to experience the reality of life from an early age, without censorship or the confines of strict parental authority.

Dad taught me to believe in myself. I only have to look at my children, strong, confident and amazing people, to know it was more than just a lesson for me.

Part Two

FAMILY HISTORY

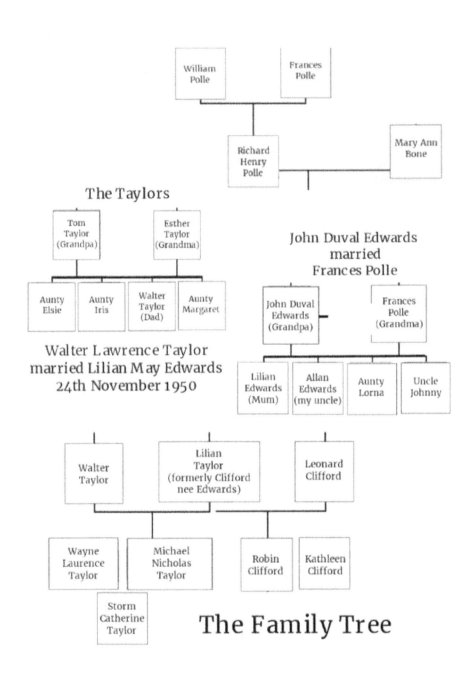

The Taylors

Walter Lawrence Taylor
married Lilian May Edwards
24th November 1950

John Duval Edwards
married
Frances Polle

The Family Tree

104

CHAPTER FIFTEEN

THE TAYLORS

My great-grandparents Charlotte and Frank Taylor

"You're such a Taylor," Mum would growl at me, whenever I annoyed her.

I believe I have strong traits from both parents, but I concede Dad and I were much alike. We both liked solitude and didn't always need someone with us to enjoy ourselves. We loved poetry, books and films, and enjoyed discussing them. In a social gathering we were often the focus of attention; loud, a little obnoxious and ready with a good joke or two.

Soon after launching into researching our family history I met Dad's cousin, Ken Foreman, a wonderful old gentleman in his nineties and as spritely as ever. He was also researching the family history and writing a book with a beautiful title: *The Light of Other Days*. We shared information, but Ken was able to give me a more personal insight into the Taylor family and its disturbing susceptibility to tragedy and alcohol dependence.

The first of our Taylors to settle in South Australia was Thomas John Taylor, his wife Elizabeth and their daughter Emma. In 1852, they left England to begin a new life in South Australia. For the first fifteen years they were doing well, having five more children: Elizabeth, Fanny, Frank, Esther and the youngest Miriam, who was affectionately called Minnie.

In 1868, and at 42 years of age, Elizabeth suddenly died. With the loss of his wife, Thomas was faced with having to care for his family alone. It would be wonderful to say he harnessed his pain and rose to the challenge. Instead, he sank into the numbing effects of alcohol and allowed the family to drift apart.

As soon as he was old enough Frank, my great-grandfather, got an apprenticeship and moved to the beach suburb of Glenelg, escaping the city and the dark, gathering clouds of familial despair. He married an English girl, Charlotte Whitehead, and went on to have ten children.

Two of them died early in childhood but the others seemed to do well, including my grandfather Tom. Ken remembered his grandparents as being wonderful people and their lives untainted by alcohol abuse. Frank's sisters weren't so fortunate.

Of the five girls only Emma was spared the brunt of the family's misfortune, having married early in the year her mother died. It would be the only wedding which would be celebrated with parents and all of her siblings. With three of her siblings still needing care, she took Esther into her home.

In 1876, when Fanny was married, their father's first name was absent and notably changed on the marriage certificate to John Taylor. By then, Thomas had clocked up charges of vagrancy and drunkenness.

Fanny found happiness in her marriage to Edwin Bayfield, a bold adventurer, explorer and hotelier. His obituary resonated with the exciting life Fanny shared with him.

Edwin Henry Bayfield

Mr. Edwin Henry Bayfield, a very old colonist died at his residence in Nairne on Monday. He was born in Currie Street on the 22nd February 1845 and was educated at Mictons Walkerville School. When quite a young man he left with the overland telegraph line workers for the Northern Territory and went through to Darwin. He saw the first cablegram that came through from England. On the last voyage of the "Gothenburg" he rode day and night through the bush to catch the vessel but was not successful. He was on the Gympie Goldfields in Queensland and was fairly successful. On his return he became licensee of the Millers Arms, Nairne where he remained for twelve years. He then took the Commercial Hotel, Two Wells for another twelve years and thence he went to the Travellers Rest at Houghton for thirteen years. Here his eyesight failed but after several operations he partly recovered his sight. Having a private residence at Nairne, he went back there about eight years ago and resided there 'til his death. He was an old member of the Manchester Unity Oddfellows Lodge of Nairne. His widow survives him.

- "The Advertiser" December 11th 1918

Missing from the obituary was any mention of children. For whatever reason, Fanny and Edwin didn't have any of their own, but they did raise a child and gave him their name. Alexander Bayfield was born Alexander Brown and was the son of Fanny's sister Esther.

I was fascinated to see another child of a Taylor woman raised by a sibling. Esther Taylor was nineteen when she married Alexander Brown senior in Sydney. The marriage didn't last long after their son's birth. Esther returned to South Australia, divorced and unable to support her son.

Unlike me, it seems Alex Junior had some knowledge of his birth parents. When he got married at the age of nineteen, his real father was named on the marriage certificate. When his second daughter was born, she was given the surname Bayfield-Brown. By 1927, Alexander and his family were living with his mother Esther, widowed by the death of her second husband. Alexander kept the name Bayfield until he died in 1964.

The youngest of the Thomas Taylor's daughters, Minnie, was only five when she lost her mother. Her sister Elizabeth accepted the responsibility of raising her and Minnie came to think of Elizabeth as her mother. When Elizabeth married John Lapthorne, Minnie was just an addition to their eight children.

Of all the Taylor women, Elizabeth suffered the hardest with the loss of three children, two who died in the same year. Minnie was an enormous support to her through these tragedies and Elizabeth was lost without her. They were devoted to one another.

Minnie was married in 1890 and moved to Wallaroo, a country town on South Australia's Yorke Peninsula. At over 160 kilometres distance, visiting was a rare option in those days. After twenty-seven years together, Elizabeth was left heartbroken without her.

Like her father, she found solace in a bottle and fell deeply into depression. Her marriage was breaking down and she had taken to sleeping in the bedroom with her eldest daughter. Within two years without her beloved sister, the pain became too much and Elizabeth ended her life at the age of 39 years.

An inquest was held in which her husband spoke of her depression. "She was constantly saying that she would be better off dead than alive."

Her 18 year-old daughter Eleanor reported that her mother had come home that day in low spirits and they had retired at 9.20pm. Next morning at 7.o'clock, it was Eleanor who found her. I can't imagine her horror and despair, but she was far from alone in her grief.

When the news reached Minnie, she was inconsolable. Soon after her own health began to falter and within a few years, and at the age of 34, she passed away. Her body was returned to the family home and she was buried in the same grave as her sister.

Less than a year after losing his daughter Elizabeth, Thomas John at the age of 66, gave up his struggle with life. In his last moments his grief and shame may have been overwhelming. Did he regret his decision to bring his family to South Australia?

Over thirty years I've searched for an obituary or a post in the newspapers, anything which might have paid him tribute. The most I could find was a mention of him in a newspaper notice announcing the marriage of one of Emma's daughters. It read 'granddaughter of Thomas Taylor, esquire of Brighton, England.' It was as if his existence in South Australia had never happened.

By the generation of his great-grandchildren, little was known of him other than what Ken had found in his research. The family didn't speak of him. Only his son Frank paid tribute by naming my grandfather Tom.

I still make random searches trying to uncover anything about our Thomas John Taylor. Being such a common name, research can only be done with the appropriate records to back it up and I've spent quite a considerable amount obtaining them, just to make sure I have the right Thomas John.

What records can't tell me is what kind of person he was; who he might have been if his wife had lived, if life had been fairer. Were there any other factors or mental disorders which might have contributed to his downfall? If family history has taught me anything, it's in being slow to judge anyone without having walked a mile in their footsteps. We are more than a product of genetics. We are shaped by history and circumstance.

Well overdue is a tribute to that first generation of our Taylors in South Australia, and so it is my privilege to write one.

To Thomas John and his wife Elizabeth, parents to one son and five daughters, grand-parents to a minimum of 32 grandchildren and 57 great-grandchildren. May they rest in peace and in the legacy they established, the happy and successful lives of their descendants, including my own.

My great-grandmother
Charlotte Taylor with my
cousin Ken Foreman

Grandparents Tom and
Esther Taylor

Aunty Margaret and Grandma

CHAPTER SIXTEEN

POLLES AND EDWARDS

My grandparents Frances Elizabeth Polle
and John Duval Edwards with Mum (1917)

Throughout my research I've often shed tears for my ancestors upon discovering their stories of tragedy and loss. None have fascinated and affected me more than those of my female forebears.

Mum was my role model of everything loving, kind and gentle but a ferocity when it came to protecting her family. Every morning without fail she dressed well, did her make-up and hair and donned an apron. By late afternoon, with the housework done and dinner cooking, she was well under the influence of booze.

Whether she was sober or drunk, we never went without good meals, made beds and clean clothes. Everything was ironed, right down to our underwear. Friday was always baking day, ensuring tins full of cakes, biscuits and tarts. She lived by strict routine which enabled her to function.

In the evenings she allowed herself to be a little more carefree while awaiting Dad's arrival home from work. Michael and I were left to our own devices and we got up to all sorts of mischief. There was no bedtime for us until we were ready to go to bed. Often we fell asleep in front of the television and Dad would put us to bed when he got home.

Mum taught me to count my blessings, to reflect often and appreciate every good moment. In spite of tragedy and an incredibly hard life, she never saw herself as a victim. Knowing her story, I can't imagine how she rose above it. I don't think I could have survived and reached my sunset years with such peace and contentment.

I can only conclude that Mum had inherited the same tenacity of the women who had gone before her, women who were equally familiar with suffering and hardship. I came to understand that within the lives of my mother, grandmother and great-grandmother was a reoccurring theme of loss, abuse and alcohol dependence. But no matter what life threw at them, these incredibly resilient, fierce women battled on and kept getting up every time they were knocked down.

Like me, Mum never knew her maternal grandmother. Mary Ann Maria Bone had abandoned her husband and four children when my grandmother was just a child. I am still trying to discover what became of her, but it didn't take much to find her tragic history.

She was sixteen when she married Mum's grandfather, Richard Henry Polle, son of a German immigrant and an English mother.

Born in 1875, Mary Ann was the eldest of six children. At the age of twelve she was already in trouble with the law for disruptive behaviour. She was eventually taken into the State Children's Department with her five-year old brother Reuben, where they were separated. Mary Ann was fostered by the family of her future husband, Richard Henry Polle.

The Polle family had experienced overwhelming tragedy of their own with only three of thirteen children alive at the time of Mary Ann's arrival. Another younger girl, May, was already living with them, having been adopted by William and Frances Polle at the age of 18 months. Soon after Mary Ann's intake William made the sudden decision to move his family to an industrial town 200 kilometres away, possibly to seek employment.

It was there Mary Ann became pregnant to Richard at the age of fifteen and was married off to him soon after the baby's birth. Richard took his young bride back to his hometown and, soon after, Mary Ann learned of the death of her brother Reuben at the age of nine due to heart failure. She was pregnant with her second son.

My grandmother was born two years later. When Mary Anne was pregnant with her fourth child, she lost her mother who was not yet fifty. By the age of twenty-two, Mary Anne was an orphan and a mother to four children and bitterly familiar with tragedy. The extent of what else she may have suffered only came to light when the most horrific secret of my family history was uncovered.

May, her foster sister, fell pregnant at the age of thirteen and again at fifteen. I was sickened to later discover both children had been fathered by Mary Anne's father-in-law, William Polle. It had me wondering whether Mary Anne's first child had been Richard's son or that of his father. When May and Mary Anne were arrested for drunkenness and lewd behaviour, May and her children were taken away to become State wards.

It seemed my great-great grandmother, Frances Polle, had turned a blind eye to her husband's perversion. If she was revolted by his actions, there was no evidence of it. She kept his memory honoured yearly with loving memorials in the newspaper. This, even after William had made numerous attempts to contact May and send her love notes. Even after being ordered by the court to stay away.

For all his crimes, the only punishment he received was being fined five shillings for disobeying a court order. May wasn't so lucky. After being raped repeatedly from the age of twelve, she then had to suffer incarceration and the loss of her children.

Guilt finally caught up with the old reprobate. William tried to take his life twice, and on his third attempt in 1905 he succeeded.

Richard's older sister either never knew or chose not to acknowledge what her father had done. Two years after his death she posted a memoriam which read:

In loving memory of my father William Polle:

If I had been there in the hour of death,
To catch the last sigh of his dying breath,
His last goodbye I might have heard
Or breathed in his ear, one parting word.

Markedly absent from the death notices was any tribute from Richard. By then he was a single father of four. For whatever tragic reason, Mary Ann was homeless and making her living on the streets, having reunited with May. These two poor women soon came up before the courts for drunken behaviour and prostitution and, once again, May was incarcerated. The court appearance was the last news I ever found out about my great-grandmother.

One of Richard and Mary Ann's children was my grandmother, Frances Elizabeth Polle. What a horrendous start to life. She was only three when her mother left. Her father eventually remarried and moved them to Port Adelaide which boasted of more pubs in one area than any other district. Many wharf workers and mariners were raising their families there while making their meagre living.

By the age of seventeen my grandmother was unmarried and pregnant to John Duval Edwards, a tall, fair-haired and tattooed Master Mariner who worked on the ketches. They were still unmarried when the baby was born, a little boy who passed away eight months later. Within a year Frances was pregnant again and they finally tied the knot, just a few short months before Mum was born.

With the outbreak of World War I my grandparents were separated. John had gone off to fight in one the bloodiest arenas of conflict in history. He was discharged medically unfit in 1917 and had to return to his life as a mariner and a family man, with another child on the way. His return must have been an enormous relief to my grandmother who had lost both her brothers in the War that year.

Mum had often spoken of her parents with a grin, saying they had fought and argued as passionately as they'd loved each other. She spoke of how her father favoured Mum above her younger sister and two younger brothers, and was often taken out on the ketch with him. It was a hard life in a bad place and alcohol was easily obtained.

As the eldest child Mum took on the role of helping to raise her brothers and sister which meant leaving school at the age of ten. When she was thirteen the family was visited by the State Child Department because of child neglect, fighting and boozing. All four children were taken away and placed with other family members. Mum was sent to Victoria to live with her aunt Myrtle and Uncle Edgar who were Salvation Army Officers. My grandfather took up extra work on the ketches and my grandmother was left to drink away her misery over the loss of her family.

Mum loved her Aunt Myrtle but didn't like to be left alone with Uncle Edgar. Myrtle decided Mum should accompany her as she did outreach work among the prostitutes in the city. Mum was only fourteen when she was helping her attend women who had self-aborted pregnancies to go on working or avoid bringing a child into their harsh, cruel world. Many of them died from infection.

Mum witnessed poverty and humanity at its worst. It gave her an understanding of the plight of women and brought about her faith in God. She became a uniformed member of the Salvation Army. For a couple of years she had some semblance of a good, stable life, but she longed to return to her parents and siblings.

What she never knew during her time away was what was happening back home. It was a discovery I made years after Mum had passed away, and I was sad at being unable to share it with her. She would have been amused despite its sinister premise.

'Alleged intent to murder' read the headline for a story reported in most newspapers around Australia. I was stunned by this discovery. My research into it gave me a real sense of my grandparents and things Mum had told me about them. She adored her parents in spite of their shortcomings, and loved reminiscing about how much they were in love with each other. Her memories were always of two wonderful people who got a little carried away when they were drinking.

115

At nearly six feet tall, my grandfather was a big tattooed man. Grandma Frances was a petite woman with a gentle nature and a fierce temper when provoked. John spent much of his time away at sea while Frances raised the children and drank. Upon John's return there was always a passionate reunion of husband and wife until the booze continued to flow.

In 1929, and with their children fostered out to various homes, my grandparents were living apart, having been ordered to do so by the court. John was living on a ketch and Frances was visiting him so they could drink together. On this particular occasion things got out of hand as this newspaper article tells us:

Saturday 29th June 1929.

Alleged Intent to Murder

John Duval Edwards, a seaman of Port Adelaide, was charged with having on June 20th pushed his wife, Frances Elizabeth Edwards, into Port Adelaide River with intent to murder her.

The prosecutor said that Edwards and his wife had been living apart, but had met at Port Adelaide that evening. They went on board a ketch. Mrs Edwards left at about 8.30 p.m., and about two hours later, returned to fetch her handbag. The defendant went on board, inquiring for his wife, who was talking to a man name McGuire. The defendant, it was alleged, pushed his wife into the river. McGuire grabbed the woman, but was unable to pull her out. Edwards went to his assistance and rescued her.

The defendant, it was alleged, had said to the police, "She is my wife, but she means nothing to me. The river is the best place for her."

Mrs Edwards said that she had fell into the water.

Recalled, she said: "My husband did not push me into the river. He put his hands on my shoulders and I lost my balance and fell in."

Edwards reserved his defence and was committed for trial. Bail was allowed.

Within a month it became obvious a conviction would never see the light of day. The police didn't regard my grandfather to be of any risk to her safety and didn't oppose bail. John was out of jail immediately and they were back seeing each other. My grandmother was deemed a 'hostile witness' by the prosecution for her firm stance of denying any wrongdoing on John's part.

The family was eventually reunited during the harsh years of economic depression, but before long my grandfather was back in the newspapers. This time it was for something a little heroic. While several miles out at sea, a fire broke out in the engine room of his ketch. Grandpa went in alone and fought the fire and his bravery made front page of many newspapers. *The Daily News* in Perth reported:

"He quelled the blaze before the ship was seriously damaged, broke his way through the smoke and fumes to the deck and, unable to smother his burning clothes, jumped into the sea."

But Grandpa's heroic deed came at great cost. He was forced to endure horrific pain until they were able to get him back to shore and then throughout the months in hospital. A third of his body was severely burned and half his face had melted away.

Mum smiled sadly whenever she spoke of that time. "He wasn't easy to look at but his good side was still as handsome as ever. It made no difference to my mother. She just loved him as she always had and was constantly at this side caring for him."

Somehow, and less than a year later, Grandpa returned to work on the ketches, but more bad times were ahead for my grandparents. There were rumours of another outbreak of war and in 1939 their fears were confirmed. Having lost both brothers to the First World War, it must have weighed heavily upon my grandmother when the eldest of her two sons, Allan Alfred Edwards, signed up to join the army in 1940. On the 1st March 1941, the entire family were at the wharves to wave goodbye as Allan disembarked for Singapore. It was the last they ever saw of him.

In 1943 my grandparents received news Allan was missing in action. It was months of anxious waiting until they were told of his internment as a prisoner-of-war in Burma. By the end of 1944 their prayers and hopes were crushed with the news of Allan's death. They received a brief summary of his drowning at sea and learned a little more from returning soldiers who had survived.

In recent years I had access to a more detailed account of Allan's death as documents were released to the public and old soldiers began to share their stories, several in which Mum's brother was mentioned.

On the 12th September 1944 Allen was a prisoner-of-war aboard the Japanese transport ship Rakuyō Maru. After months of starvation, torture and being forced to work on the infamous Burma to Thailand railway, he was barely more than a skeleton. For six days he was crammed in with a thousand other prisoners, in a space barely able to accommodate three hundred and rife with disease and human waste. It's easy to see why these ships were given the more ominous title of 'hell-ship.'

In the early hours of the morning the ship was torpedoed by an American submarine and began to sink. Allan was alive when he went into the water, covered in oil and clinging to anything to keep afloat, but malnutrition and dysentery had left him too weak to hold on and he eventually drowned. He was only 24 years old.

"He was the good one," Mum would say of him. "Robin adored his Uncle Allan. He should never have died like that."

His death always haunted Mum and his portrait was one of the few framed pictures of family displayed in our home. After several drinks and in her darkest melancholic moments, Uncle Allan was often remembered with tears.

It is impossible to imagine how this family survived so much grief. Grandpa died two years before I was born, falling asleep in a chair while reading the paper. Grandma followed him a few years later, having deeply grieved his loss throughout that time. I was a year old when she died and I'm only sorry I didn't get a chance to know my grandparents.

Looking at Mum's family and these three generations of women, I feel their flaws lie in the shadow of their courage and resilience. I only wish Mum, Grandma and Great-Grandma could see my two beautiful daughters; strong, confident women at the helm of their lives, raising their families and pursuing their goals with enormous success. I'm sure they would be as proud as I am.

CHAPTER SEVENTEEN

THE TALE OF TWO DAUGHTERS

To the old rugged cross I will ever be true,
Its shame and reproach gladly bear.
Then He'll call me someday to my home far away
Where his glory forever I'll share.

The Old Rugged Cross - George Bennard (1873–1958).

When I took my Mum to the hospital on a wet Tuesday night, suffering from bad indigestion, I was shattered to be told her discomfort was due to having suffered a massive heart attack. By the following Saturday it had robbed us of her life. The registrar had looked at me curiously. "Surely she must have had experienced terrible pain at some stage."

I could only shrug. If she had, Mum hadn't said anything. Pain wasn't something Mum thought worth mentioning more than an occasional grumble.

They wanted to admit her to the palliative care ward but I refused. One of the few desires Mum had often mentioned in her life was to die in her own bed, the one in which she had spent a thirty-eight year marriage with Dad. For a woman who had asked for very little in life, it was a desire I was determined to fulfil.

In her last few days she was peaceful and happy. The morphine had given her an unexpected respite from the cruel thirty-year affliction of rheumatoid arthritis. There was no fear of death. She had faith in God and yearned for a reunion with Dad in the afterlife. I can honestly say she was the happiest dying person I'd ever known.

She was surrounded by those she loved, and encouraged my kids to come into her bedroom to talk with her. Her joy was complete with the arrival of Robin. I was the only one not coping.

One night I crawled into bed with her and cuddled up to her, just as I had done as a child. I wanted to make sure everything which needed to be said had its moment, but she stopped me.

119

There was nothing she needed to hear from me. She knew she was loved and there were no wounds to heal or regrets. We'd had a great life together and as far as she was concerned her 78 years had been blessed with nothing but love and happiness. The past was what it was, and there was nothing which needed resolving, at least not with me and Robin. We spoke about Michael and she made me promise to tell him how much he was loved if I ever found him.

Only one of her children struggled to find peace. Kathleen arrived at our house, stylishly dressed and straining to remain unemotional. Having only seen her a few times in my life, she was still very much a stranger and I was wary of her. Previous encounters had left Mum in tears and I wasn't about to let anyone upset her.

Mum was thrilled to see her. As Kathleen sat down on the bed she suddenly crumpled in tears, telling Mum how sorry she was while explaining away the years of estrangement. My resentment turned to pity as I saw how broken she was.

Mum patted her hand and insisted she had nothing to be sorry about. If there was any blame to be laid, it was hers. I was content to leave them alone to talk. She was red-eyed and weary when she came out of the bedroom. For the next hour she sat and talked with me and Robin.

"I never knew her," she explained. "I could only go by what Dad and Enid had told me. It was years before I knew the truth, and even then I felt as if I would be betraying my dad if I contacted her. When he died too much time had passed, and I couldn't face her for years. All that time she was thinking of me. Did you know she has my baby booties, and newspaper clippings of my engagement and wedding, even the births of my boys?"

Of course I knew. Kathleen wasn't entirely a stranger to me. A huge black and white portrait had sat on Mum's dresser for as long as I could remember, featuring a pretty little blonde girl with a ribbon in her hair. I was told on many occasions how Kathleen was a matron in a hospital and married to a doctor.

I had first met Kathleen when Robin was staying with us during his leave from the Navy. I was about seven years old and he had treated me to a wonderful day at Marine Land and the Lion Park. We'd got stuck there for over an hour because a huge male lion had jumped into the back of the ute and refused to get out.

On our way home Robin was unusually quiet and suddenly turned off from the highway. He drove out to an unfamiliar suburb and a large, upscale and fine looking house. I remember feeling a little intimidated.

He had warned me along the way that the people we were visiting might act a bit odd, and they certainly did. The woman who let us in was friendly enough after her initial shock, but her tall, lean husband had a stern face with a downturned mouth. His outright glare at me was the only interchange we had.

I was awed by another woman, a beautiful young blonde who also kept staring at me and tentatively offered me some biscuits and milk. There was a collective gasp and gazes of shock when I asked for a cup of tea instead.

Fortunately, the dog really liked me and I happily spent the next hour playing out in the garden with him. Occasionally I heard raised voices inside and was stunned to hear Robin getting angry. He suddenly came out to me, gathered me up in his arms and strode back to the car. We drove away silently. I let him calm down before I dared to ask who those people were.

He was hesitant in replying, probably uncertain of how much I knew about the peculiarities of our family.

"The blonde lady is my sister Kathy, and the older couple... He's my dad and Enid is my stepmother."

I nodded knowingly. "Oh okay. Mum and Dad told me about them. Can we go back to the lion park one day?"

The second time I met Kathy was many years later just after the birth of Lee. It was a Saturday, race day, and routine wasn't something easily interrupted in our lives. Everything that afternoon was weird.

In the morning Dad and I wheeled my son in his pram to the TAB and placed our bets, before I headed back to my flat to do some washing. I returned to my parents' house at lunchtime and immediately noticed the flash car parked out front. I was curious but annoyed, knowing how much my parents hated visitors.

I wheeled the pram inside and heard a stranger's voice instead of the familiar chatter of the racing commentators. The next shock was entering the kitchen and finding my parents sober and no sign of their flagon of port.

The blonde lady was sitting at the table talking with Mum. Dad was looking sour as he made a pot of tea. The best china was out on the table along with the tablecloth which only came out at Christmas. Kathy greeted me warmly and made polite endearments about my baby.

I reluctantly joined the awkward gathering and noticed how nervous Kathy was. She kept glancing about the room, noting the smoke-yellowed walls, the old mismatched furniture, the curtain replacing the missing door to the bathroom and the strips of mat on the faded linoleum.

Mum did most of the talking while Dad and I exchanged impatient glances wondering how our racehorses were faring. When Kathy finally got up to leave, Dad waited until Mum had escorted her out before firing up the radio and filling his glass with port. Upon Mum's return we both got a sound telling off for not trying hard enough to make her feel welcome.

When she got tearful we consoled her and promised to try harder the next time, but there was no next time. It would be another ten years before we would see her again.

After Dad died I contacted Kathy hoping to bring some happiness back into Mum's life while continuing my foray into our family history. The visit didn't turn out as I'd hoped.

Kathleen's home was in a prestigious suburb and her beautiful house was filled with classy, expensive furniture. I felt some resentment, having grown up in rented houses, secondhand clothes, with few luxuries or even the basic assets like a car and an indoor toilet.

That day Mum met her grandsons for the first time – two stunningly tall, handsome lads who had inherited Mum's dark features. They were polite but I could see they had little idea of who this woman was to them. The whole visit was stilted and uncomfortable. I don't know how she kept it together that day, but she didn't fall apart until I drove away from the house.

I was furious as I pulled over and held her, despising anyone who could hurt her or treat her with contempt. It was so unfair. For far too long Mum had accepted the blame of being absent from Kathy's life.

At Mum's funeral, Kathy seated herself in the back rows until I made her come sit up front with me. By then I was sad for this woman, well into her fifties and comprehending an enormous loss in an otherwise successful life. Those important family events which could have been shared with her

122

mother were lost and irretrievable. Her sons would never know their grandmother.

It was seeing Kathy in that last week, I understood how much richer I was for having had what she'd missed out on - a life shared with Mum. It was me who had the exclusive privilege of caring for her in those last years and in her final days. It was my children she had held in her arms and loved so dearly. It was their birthdays and Christmas she'd celebrated. It was my wedding at which she beamed with pride, watching me marry Andrew and on the very same day, thirty-four years earlier, when she'd married Dad.

Robin and I had many conversations about her. Kathy was only seven years-old when she was taken away from Mum. The same fate might have befallen Robin had he not rebelled against his father by running away to join the Navy. He had to lie about his age of fifteen to be accepted into the career he held for forty years. When on leave, his time was always spent with us.

Kathy had only her father's version of the marriage breakdown. As far as she knew, Mum had deserted her family for another man. The truth and its tragic consequences were not known to her for years. Robin's attempt to set her straight only strained their relationship. Some time spent with Mum would have shown Kathy the kind of woman she was. Mum never gave up any child willingly. She was full of love and truly remarkable. One only had to look at the full house on the day of her funeral.

Many members of the Salvation Army were there in uniform and one man played her favourite hymn on a harmonica. Everyone managed to keep it together until my eldest daughter, nine years old at the time, got up and read a beautiful poem she had written for Mum. We still laugh about how the place was reduced to weeping. Mum would have been amused.

The words spoken at the funeral would have resonated in Kathy's heart. A lot of people shared how much Mum meant to them and what an incredible woman she was.

I haven't seen Kathy since that day, and now another twenty-five years have passed. I don't expect to see her again. We spent an hour on the phone when Robin passed away. She's a widow now and her sons are doing well, one as a professional golfer. I still feel an attachment to her. We were both daughters to Mum, one adopted and the other born to her, living such vastly different lives. What we shared equally was the love of our mother.

CHAPTER EIGHTEEN

FAMILY AT WAR

If life wasn't hard enough, my parents had to deal with two World Wars and the impact of both on their families. Mum was born in 1916 during the First World War which had claimed the lives of two uncles and thankfully spared her father. The years which followed were tough growing up in Port Adelaide, the eldest of four children subjected to the volatile behaviour of their parents.

She knew nothing of her parents' 'attempted murder' drama. By the age of eighteen she had an active social life and was being courted by many young men who took her dancing at the Maris Palais in Semaphore.

It was at that time she met Leonard Clifford, a man twelve years her senior and a recent immigrant from England. After a brief time together, she fell pregnant to him and they had to be married quickly.

Len wasn't fond of Mum's parents and whisked his new bride off to his parents' house in Parkside. A few short months later, on the 9th November 1935, Robin Wilfred Duval Clifford was born to them.

While Mum was devoted to being a mother, her role as a devoted wife was much more challenging. Her husband didn't share her philosophy of gentleness and instead, believed in strict discipline.

Determined to change Mum's social habits, he insisted upon a quiet, respectable life. Mum hated being so far away from her parents. Without a car or licence, public transport meant a three-hour journey there and back to visit them.

A young couple with a child lived across the road and Mum became friends with the mother, Gladys. Len got on well with her husband and was satisfied to spend time with him when Mum and Gladys took the children out.

In those years in which Mum lived with us, I found letters from Gladys dated 1950. Mum had fond memories of her, prompting me to locate Gladys and call her. Her response was tearful, excited and eager to see her dear friend.

Mum was quite nervous as I drove her out to Gladys' home, but she had no need for worry. Their reunion after forty years was something extraordinary. These women in their seventies became like young girls again, laughing, talking over each other and recalling memory after memory. I was privileged to share in this time with them, listening and recording their stories of fun, mischief and despair.

It provided me with a detailed account of some of Mum's darkest days. At first Gladys held back from saying much about Mum's marriage to Len and the events which followed. When I assured her I was aware of most of it, Gladys seemed eager to speak and expressed her sorrow and regret at not having supported Mum when she needed a friend. As usual, Mum brushed off her concerns and wanted to talk about the good times.

"We always told them we were going to the pictures," Gladys beamed, her comment followed by a chuckle from Mum. "But we weren't. We were going to the pubs and sometimes we took the children. During the summer, we stayed with Lil's parents so we could take the children to the beach, and they would look after them so we could go dancing.

"Your mother was a beautiful young woman and men were always trying to talk to her. That's where your Dad was different from all the others, and very different from Len. He was a real gentleman. It was easy to see why Lil fell in love with him."

Gladys remembered Len as a stern, sober man, very hard on Robin and disapproving of Mum's family. He was an active member of the Freemasons and expected Mum to attend elite social gatherings and be on her best behaviour. He was determined to present a respectable family and an obedient wife. Robin often suffered harsh discipline to ensure he was seen as the well-behaved son. Often, Mum would intervene to protect Robin and end up suffering the consequences.

"Your mother always did her best," Gladys continued. "She kept a beautiful home, did extraordinary needlework and dressmaking, baked and cooked and made sure dinner was on the table for Len in the evenings, but it was never enough. Robin was a lovely boy, well-dressed, good manners and very quiet whenever his father was around. He was very different when he was alone with Lil, laughing and mischievous and so much happier. He adored your Mum, loved her parents and when Wally came along, he adored him."

She remembered the Taylor family living down the road. "We had to go past the house to get to the main road to catch the bus. We'd occasionally see Wally. He was just a young lad then and he would give us a nod, but he'd be staring at your mother. But then the War came along and everything changed for us."

Len joined the Army and Mum went home to be with her parents. Their lives were much quieter and Mum was able to enjoy watching them dote upon Robin, but the time was brief. In 1942 Len was discharged from the Army and Mum had to return to the house in Parkside.

Soon after, she fell pregnant with Kathleen and was constantly ill and suffering from anaemia. Her mother came to stay and help out with Robin, while Mum was confined to bedrest. Kathleen was born in June 1943 and Grandma Edwards stayed on while Mum recovered from a difficult birth, which had left her gravely ill. It had been a year since her brother Allan had become 'missing-in-action' and no news was forthcoming.

Len had taken up employment as a travelling salesman and was away from home for long periods. It was a relief for Mum as the marriage had already begun to break down soon after Kathleen's birth. She was tired of his mirthless demeanour, his disapproval of her family and his regimental discipline of Robin. As soon as she was recovered, Mum was out enjoying herself again with the children and her best friend, Gladys.

Kathleen had just turned two when the family received news of Allan's death. While the news was a crushing blow to the family, it was just the beginning of years of sorrow for Mum.

While still grieving for her brother, she became aware her husband was keeping company with a young girl. He had taken another job as a taxi driver and was away from home more than ever. Mum realised how little she cared. Life was easier without him and she had Gladys and the children to keep her company.

Meanwhile, Dad had been away for years with the Army, doing active duty in Indonesia. He fought in the Battle of Balik Papan, one of the last campaigns of the War. When surrender came in August 1945 many of his

126

friends had died. The thought of returning to civilian life was daunting. When an opportunity arose for soldiers to volunteer for work in the Occupation of Japan, Dad was quick to sign up. His time spent there gave him a deep appreciation for the country and the people.

It was tragedy which brought him home having received news his father was dying of bowel cancer. By the time he got home his father had passed away, leaving his mother grief-stricken.

It wasn't the homecoming he'd hoped for. His two older sisters Elsie and Iris were married and living interstate. His youngest sister Margaret had just got married and was expecting her first child. Dad was the only one without commitments, which meant moving back in with his mother to care for her. He got a job as a barman at the nearby Waverley Hotel. While the pay wasn't good, the job provided a social life and a chance to meet a girl.

One afternoon a young woman came into the saloon where he was working. Dad recognised her as the woman who had often passed by his house with her little boy. She was drinking heavily and a crowd of men were vying for her attention. Dad quickly strode up to order the men to back off. His imposing presence defied anyone to challenge him, but he was no match for Mum. She was flirty, defiant and opinionated, and Dad could see trouble looming. He finally told her to drink up and he would personally walk her home.

Along the way they became good friends, sharing similar burdens of friends and loved ones lost during the War. Mum's visits to the pub became more frequent, as did their slow walks back home.

For the first time since returning home, Dad had someone who took his mind off the things he had seen during the War, memories which would haunt his dreams to the end of his days. Mum was different from other women; beautiful, funny and light-hearted about life. It bothered him to be so fond of her knowing she was married with children.

One night as he walked her home, it was obvious she was having some difficulty walking in her stiletto heels after several red wines in her system. She then made him a proposal which Dad always spoke about with a chuckle and a long gaze of love at Mum.

"Piggyback me."

And he did, laughing and talking all the way home. When he finally set her down outside her home, she smiled softly and her gaze lingered on his face. Dad knew right then and there they had both fallen deeply in love.

After surviving the devastation of war Dad was about to face another conflict, one in which there was no training or comrades to fight with him. He would be fighting for the woman he loved.

CHAPTER NINETEEN

LOVE STORY

Mum and Dad

During the first two years of my marriage, Andrew got to know my parents well. Every Thursday night we went to their house for dinner and Andrew would bring Dad a few beers, especially if he wanted to chat with him. When sober Dad was a man of few words, but a couple of drinks always got him talking while he cooked.

By then Mum was badly crippled with rheumatoid arthritis. Her fingers had become severely deformed and the swelling in her knees and feet made walking difficult. Every so often she had cortisone and gold injections which brought short periods of relief. Most of the time she suffered pain and needed strong medication and sleeping pills to allow her some sleep.

Mum refused to give in and continued her normal routine, doing her hair, applying a little make-up and donning her apron. Dad, however, wouldn't allow her to do half as much as she wanted. Every day he was up early, making her breakfast in bed and getting most of the housework done before she could attempt it.

He took over the grocery shopping, laundry and the cooking as well, much to Mum's annoyance. In the evening he made her put her feet up and gave her a hot water bottle to keep her warm while he massaged her knees and feet with some heating balm. Mum was rarely drinking then, but occasionally they would have an afternoon together with a bottle of port to relive some of those earlier days.

On one occasion, Andrew took Mum and Dad home after they'd been drinking at our place. He was worried Mum had drunk too much and Dad would need help looking after her. Instead, he was promptly dismissed at the front door and encouraged to leave. I laughed when he came home and told me. I explained how my parents were still very amorous, especially after a few drinks. While Andrew's parents had sometimes displayed affection for each other, my parents were often openly passionate.

Growing up I witnessed many playful moments between them, or Mum sitting on Dad's lap. There were loving gazes and gentle kisses and rarely any arguments. I saw Mum hit Dad with a frying pan once but he simply shrugged it off. Another time he came home drunk with his friend, Tom, wanting to bring him inside to drink. Mum was out the front watering the garden and she stopped them at the front gate. Tom was told to go home but Dad argued to bring him in, until Mum turned the hose on both of them, saturating them from head to foot.

During my time within their thirty-eight years of marriage, I witnessed a love story which shaped my own ideas about relationships. Dad set a high standard of what to expect from any man who wanted to be my life partner. Such a man would have to treat me with loyalty, respect and kindness, and always with love and tenderness. He would have to make me laugh often, devote time and conversation to me, and always make me feel beautiful. I know Dad was happy with the man I chose.

My parents often spoke openly of their first years together. I think it was a need to ensure their story could never be tarnished or their love seen as anything wrong. Mum's first marriage was unhappy, long before she met Dad. It could have ended amicably, but Len's pride was hurt and he had a reputation to uphold.

When he confronted Mum about being seen with Dad, she didn't deny their affection for each other, but didn't see why it mattered, since Len had his girlfriend, Enid. But Len didn't see it that way. Mum had a duty to be faithful to him and he wanted her affair to end.

Dad was also getting rebuked by his family, especially his mother. Grandma was disgusted with her son seeing a married woman who was five years older and possibly foreign with those dark features of hers. She had never quite recovered from her eldest daughter, Elsie, marrying a Catholic.

In the midst of all the trouble, Robin and Kathleen were suffering. Mum blamed herself and decided she had a duty to stay in her marriage and try to fix it. For a while they moved out of the family home and rented a house in Norwood, possibly because Mum was less likely to run into Dad. Len, however, continued his relationship with Enid.

Life only got harder for Mum. She had no friends or support and the arguments with Len continued. At one stage while visiting her parents, her unhappiness became overwhelming. After a few drinks she wandered down to the bridge over the Port River and stood looking down into the water. Throughout her thirty-three years she had endured too much and her future looked bleak.

As she climbed up onto the railing she was seen by a couple of men who rushed to grab her. They dragged her back onto the bridge, calmed her down and took her back to her parents' house. Mum was ashamed of allowing herself to get to this point and decided she deserved some happiness and a man who loved her.

Mum found her way back to Dad and didn't care less who knew. They went out together and even took the kids for picnics and trips to the beach. Robin grew fond of his mother's special friend who knew how to have fun and lacked the strict, sober temper of his father. Even Kathy remembered Dad as a kind and gentle man.

Meanwhile, Enid was insisting upon something more permanent with Len and wanted him to divorce Mum. Len finally approached Mum with the idea of going their separate ways and she readily accepted.

In the 1950s divorce wasn't as easily obtained as it is these days. There had to be strong grounds for the dissolution of a marriage. As a respected figure in his Freemason lodge, Len had a reputation to uphold and wasn't about to admit any wrongdoing on his part. He suggested the four of them get together to discuss what they would do, and Len put a proposal to Mum and Dad.

If Mum took the blame for infidelity he would move out, pay for the divorce and let Mum have custody of the children. They could also return to the family home in Parkside and buy it for a good price.

Mum described this time as the four of them sitting around having a few drinks and calmly discussing the matter. Len was exceptionally friendly to Dad and said he would take care of all the details. Dad only ever remembered that moment with a scowl, knowing how naïve he'd been.

With evidence of infidelity needed, Len knew a couple of private detectives who would help them out. Despite what followed, Mum and Dad always still managed to laugh whenever they spoke of the night they were 'caught.'

It was all arranged. Mum and Dad went to a hotel in the city and got into bed with each other. They snuggled and giggled under the sheets while awaiting the detectives to catch them out. On cue, these two men came in through a fire-escape window which had been left opened for them. Mum and Dad had to sit up and look suitably shocked as they were caught in the flash of a camera. After that, they got out of bed and spent the next few hours having drinks with the detectives.

In the weeks that followed, it became apparent how foolish they had been. As promised, Len moved out and left her with Robin and Kathleen, but it wasn't for long. The news of their affair spread quickly. Dad was the first to suffer, getting fired from his job at the Waverly Hotel and suffering the wrath of his family.

Grandma was furious and extremely nasty towards Mum. It was during this time she pronounced the title upon Mum which followed her through her life: 'The black bitch from Birkenhead.' They were shunned by family and friends and their social life abruptly ended. Dad was even asked to leave his local Return Soldiers League, though it was said to be due to his 'communist' ethics.

For a long time they felt as if it was them against the world. It was a devastating time which had much to do with my parents becoming reclusive and distrustful of people. Through the years I lived at home with them, I rarely saw visitors.

Dad finally managed to get employment at the Hotel Richmond where he remained until retirement, twenty-seven years later. The hours were long and his wage was terrifyingly inadequate when he and Mum were summoned to appear in court. Len was armed with an expensive lawyer, whereas Mum and Dad were unable to afford any representation.

It was during that first hearing it became apparent how cruelly they'd been deceived. Len's lawyer presented a case which painted Mum as a cheating, alcoholic harlot, who had devastated her marriage and was unfit to be a mother. The lawyer further announced he would be suing for all court costs, including his own substantial fee.

With photographic evidence presented, the judgement was swift and severe. Divorce would be granted immediately and full custody of the children would be awarded to Len. Mum was to lose entitlement to any financial assistance and Dad would be fined on top of all costs incurred. Mum and Dad were crushed by the judgement and left in financial ruin for years, something from which they never recovered.

While packing up my parents' home after Dad died, I came across a cloth bag full of receipts of the payments made for divorce costs and lawyer's fees which ran into hundreds of pounds; a vast amount in those days.

While the evidence showed the financial hardship they suffered, my parents had mostly remembered that time with humour. They prided themselves in their ingenious ways of surviving, which included some occasional shoplifting. Mum once hid a frozen chicken up her dress and walked out of the shops, pretending to be pregnant. Dad pinched a whole set of crockery from a rival pub which still had the logo on every plate, dish and cup.

But within the funny stories, and the home I grew up in, were the reminders of their poverty. There was rarely anything new. Our mismatched furniture was old and worn. There was no car or phone or going away for holidays. They never owned a house, but it didn't matter. They had each other.

In the midst of this, Mum was dealing with the loss of her children and not being able to see them. However, Robin was fifteen and was not about to be parted from his mother. He was sick of his father's hateful attitude towards her and had no wish to live with him. Against his father's wishes,

133

and with the help of Mum's parents, Robin ran away and joined the Navy. It gave him independence and the ability to be with Mum whenever he wanted.

Mum was overjoyed with having her son back. Eventually, Kathy was allowed to visit, but Len's influence had done its damage. As far as Kathy was concerned, the fault lay with Mum, and Kathy had no desire to see her.

On the 24th November 1950, Mum and Dad became husband and wife in a quiet ceremony at the Registry Office in the city. It was 34 years later, on my wedding day, when Dad informed me it was the same day he had married Mum and in the very same Registry Office.

Happiness was seeping back into their lives. Not long after their wedding, Mum found out she was pregnant. Dad was thrilled, and together they prepared for the arrival of their child. Dad found old nursery furniture which he fixed and painted, while Mum knitted, sewed and embroidered a layette.

After nine months of a trouble-free pregnancy a baby boy was born, Wayne Lawrence Taylor. Mum dressed him in the garments she'd made, and there was nothing like a baby to bring some forgiveness from family and friends. People came to visit Mum in the hospital and lovely cards were sent to them.

But tragedy was never far off. Eight days later, while still in the hospital, Wayne suddenly became ill and died within hours. Mum fell apart, collapsing with grief and an illness which had slowly been taking its toll.

The diagnosis only added to their despair. Dad had Rh negative blood which had caused Mum's body to produce antibodies which had attacked the baby in the womb along with Mum's immune system. It was a condition only just being discovered in the fifties. It wasn't until the seventies that they were able to treat mothers and babies affected. The doctors told Mum and Dad that any baby born to them would suffer a similar fate and Mum's life would be put in jeopardy.

Mum needed care for months and had no choice but to return to her parent's house so Dad could keep working to pay their bills. My grandmother and great-aunt Myrtle cared for Mum during this time, but one can scarcely imagine the depth of grief she was going through.

She eventually recovered and was reunited with Dad. For the next ten years they made a life together and bitterly accepted what fate had dealt them. . .

I've reflected upon that time when Dad had to go it alone, separated from Mum, grieving for his son and knowing he would never have a child of his own. It was the perfect incentive to run away from all of it. Only six years after surviving the War, he was penniless and faced a bleak, childless future if he chose to stay with Mum. Without her, he could move on, find a new job, make some money and find someone he could have children with.

The thought never crossed his mind. Robin and I had a rather dramatic way of describing my Dad's love for Mum: He would have crawled a mile over broken glass, just to bleed in her shadow. He loved and cared for her to the end and I was thankful he had passed away before she did. He wouldn't have lasted a day before joining her, one way or another.

Dad behind the bar at the Hotel Richmond, Adelaide

CHAPTER TWENTY

AUNTY MARGARET

Dad had three sisters: Elsie and Iris who were older, and Margaret who was younger. I met Aunty Iris and Uncle Archie only once, when they made the journey from Victoria, so I remember little about them. My widowed Aunty Elsie also lived in Victoria and made several visits, but spent little time with us. There was a lot of tension with her presence.

Michael didn't like her much because she wasn't particularly friendly to either me or Michael. She did give me a pretty bracelet once, and then I found out Susan had received a whole array of gifts. I was most indignant with childish jealousy.

Mum and Dad grumbled about her visits. Mum, because she had to tolerate her and Dad, because Aunty Elsie seemed to hold him responsible for the state of Grandma's house. As usual I was always listening to their arguments.

"Why don't you do something about that bloody house?"

"It's nothing to do with me," Dad would retort. "If they want to live in a fucking pigsty, that's their business. Don't fucking come all the way here to get on my back. You and Iris fucked off years ago to get away from it."

"And what about Susan? How can you abide her growing up in that?"

"Well, if you and Mum hadn't fucking interfered, things might have been different. Or maybe if you'd stepped in when Margaret was struggling with that bastard she was married to and his fucking interfering mother. At least Lil and I were there for her."

"Margaret needed to toughen up a bit."

"How could she? She had you, Mum and that other bitch on her back all the time. She didn't have a hope. Her husband was an abusive fucking prick and all you lot kept insisting she had a duty to stay in her marriage and work it out. The whole fucking lot of you broke her, and Lil and I did our best to pick up the pieces."

Dad had never been particularly fond of his eldest sister, but approved highly of her brother-in-law. Being a horse trainer, his name was often mentioned on our Saturday race days, but it was another of Dad's accounts of this man which remained my favourite.

During the War, Dad took leave and went to stay with Elsie and her husband Fred, who were bookies for the races. Apparently, a lot of illegal and heavy-handed tactics went on with their customers. While Dad liked Fred, it was his brother George with whom he was particularly good mates.

Having saved up a good sum of money, Dad decided to use all of it to go halves with George on a 'hot tip' over a couple of horses George knew well. Both horses were at long odds and the bet, a daily double, required both horses to win their respective races to pay out.

Every time Dad recounted the story I would see his eyes glaze over, recalling the thrill of that moment when both horses came in.

"Thirty thousand pounds," he would say reverently. "That's like a million dollars now. We were rich, but I had to go back to my battalion. George, on the other hand, used his to start up his stud farm and the rest is history."

How authentic the story is, I have no idea or evidence, just Dad's word for it, and history it certainly was. George went on to become one of Australia's most famous horse-trainers with three Melbourne Cup winners. Dad paid off his parents' house and blew the rest on 'wine, women and song.'

Having met many of Dad's Army buddies, there were several stories which supported his version and spoke of Dad's generosity in sharing his winnings.

"We could have been rich, Dad," I would argue.

Dad would just shake his head. "That was the nature of war. You didn't know if you were going to make it back alive. You just lived in the moment and I don't regret any money spent on good mates."

At Dad's funeral several of them showed up in uniform and spoke about him. You could hear the love they had for him and saw their reverence as they stood quietly and saluted Dad's Australian flag–covered coffin. They wiped tears away, as we all did, when the Last Post was played and poppies were laid on the coffin. Later that day Mum received a telegram from George, sending his condolences and expressing his fond memories of a good mate.

Dad was an amazing storyteller, and it made it difficult to know which of his stories were true or slightly embellished upon. But there were many I had no doubts about, especially those concerning Aunty Margaret and the years leading up to my adoption.

By the mid-fifties, Aunty Margaret's marriage to William Peters was crumbling. An ever interfering mother-in-law was one of the biggest problems, picking on everything Margaret did. She would even come in and do the housework and bring meals for her son and grandchildren. Bill did nothing to defend his wife and always took the side of his mother.

Aunty Margaret's mother and eldest sister showed little support. They both believed it to be a woman's duty to stay in the marriage and fix it, no matter how abusive, but none of them knew the extent of what Margaret was going through.

It was only through my family research I uncovered a court record of a horrendous crime committed by William two years prior to their wedding. It gave me a clear understanding of who he was. If Margaret had known, she would have never married him. Instead, as usual, it fell upon the woman to be morally upstanding whatever abuse she was suffering.

Margaret turned to drinking and being away from the family home, spending a lot of time with Mum and Dad. One day while at a pub with her two children, she sent her young daughter across the road to buy cigarettes.

The little girl was struck by a motor cycle and sustained a substantial head injury. Though she recovered, it was the excuse Bill needed to end the marriage. In 1958 Bill was given custody of their children and promptly returned to his parents' house, leaving Margaret without any means of support. She had no choice but to move back in with Grandma.

Drinking heavily, she lamented the loss of her children. Grandma was little comfort to her, still bitter from the loss of my grandfather and likewise drinking her grief away. It was during a visit to Mum and Dad that Margaret met Robin who was on leave from the Navy. Although nine years younger than her, Robin became fond of his stepfather's sister and passion soon erupted. By 1960 Margaret was pregnant to him.

This caused all sorts of bother. Grandma still hated Mum, and Mum wasn't happy about her son being intimate with Margaret. It was a time of nasty disputes between them all. A relationship with her baby's father was also impossible with Robin's position in the Navy.

After having seen active duty during the last years of the Malayan Emergency (1948 – 1960), Robin was promoted into special operations and communications. He was involved in Top Secret operations and decoding high level signals, a position which often had our family under the scrutiny of our Aussie spy network.

Margaret knew she had no finances to bring another child into the world and suggested Mum and Dad adopt her baby. It was the dream neither of them had dared to believe in, and Mum quickly set about making arrangements with the adoption services. Once again she was knitting and sewing baby clothes, buying toys and a cot and sharing in the joy with Dad of finally becoming parents together.

Grandma was furious with Margaret for getting pregnant and even angrier over Robin being the father. Whatever happened during that time, or whatever influence Grandma held, it wasn't until the baby girl was born that things turned sour. When Mum and Dad went to collect their new addition, they were met with a stark change of mind on Margaret's part. She was keeping her baby and couldn't be persuaded otherwise.

Any mention of this time in future conversations with my parents only inspired sombre frowns and elusive answers. I can only imagine the pain they suffered, surrounded by the baby clothes Mum had made, the toys and an empty bassinet.

It was during this time Mum and Dad were approached by the Salvation Army and asked if they wanted to care for a little boy whose young mother was single and struggling to survive.

Though not permitted to adopt him, Michael was every bit their son. He was their miracle child and an answer to prayer after eleven years of loss and disappointment. Michael came into a home with two people who had an abundance of love waiting for him.

As for Margaret, she now had a child to financially support on her own, and Grandma had found distraction from her own troubles by becoming the caregiver of the new baby. When Robin was on leave again, he wanted to see his child but was denied. He even proposed marriage to Margaret but was turned down, though she remained friends with him.

Robin always believed it was Grandma who refused him access. Over the next two years he kept in touch with Margaret and spent short stints with her whenever he was on leave. It was because of this, Robin believed himself to be the father when Margaret fell pregnant again.

I've always loved Aunty Margaret. She was gentle and kind and no less a victim of society and circumstance. I know she loved Dad, and it wouldn't have been easy to see Dad suffer when he was denied her first baby girl.

After what she had been through, it seems odd that she would willingly get pregnant with me, within a year after having Susan, living with Grandma and struggling to survive. I've tried hard to find answers. Was I the result of guilt, love or misfortune? Did she feel guilty for having denied Mum and Dad their child and then purposely fallen pregnant to give them another?

Margaret remained elusive about the details of my conception and took her secret to the grave. I feel sad she didn't feel able to tell me the circumstances. It evokes dark thoughts, and I've persuaded myself to believe she had me purposely for Mum and Dad.

Days after my birth Mum and Dad came to take me home. There was no resistance from anyone, except maybe Michael who was a little peeved at having to share Mum and Dad. Eventually he came to love me.

Mum and Dad had two awesome first names waiting for me: Thor for a boy after the god of thunder and Storm for a girl, simply because Dad loved a name he'd read in a book. Margaret's wish was also honoured and I was given the middle name of Catherine. My first name took a few years to grow on me and was subject to many taunts and jokes. You can't imagine how many times I've been asked if my parents were hippies. Not hippies, just rebels, and they had to fight in the courts so I could keep my name, but that's another story. This one is Aunty Margaret's.

When Dad died Margaret grieved for her brother and I saw a chance of healing some old wounds. I began to bring Mum and Margaret together and booked them a holiday cabin down at Semaphore. Over the next three years Margaret spent many weekends with our family and I loved seeing her laughing and chatting with Mum. She even knitted some clothes when I was pregnant with our youngest son.

Sadly she never got to see him. Margaret passed away on the 16th August 1990. She spent her last weeks in the hospital during which I worked up the courage to finally ask the question which had been burning inside.

"Please, Aunty Margaret, I need to know. Is Robin my father or is it someone else?"

She shook her head. "You don't need to know. Wally was a good father, your only father."

"I know that. Dad was a great father, and I would never dishonour him, but this is about me, who I am. Please, please, Aunty Margaret, just give me a name."

Her mouth tightened and she looked away, tears in her eyes. With a deep breath she eventually spoke. "Steven Williams and that's all you're going to get. Don't ask me anything else."

I didn't. I already felt as if I'd accosted a dying woman. It was awful and I suspect Aunty Margaret said something to her children. When we tried to visit we were made unwelcomed by her children - my half-brother Phillip and elder half-sister, Helen - as if we didn't have a right to be there. I accepted their wishes and backed off quietly. A few weeks later I got a phone call to say she had died. It was a bitter moment which tore me up, feeling I'd been robbed of my chance to be there when she passed away.

At the funeral Mum and I sat and listened to people talking nonsense about this amazing woman. They tried to paint her as a saint and mentioned nothing of her true character. If I'd had a chance, or even been acknowledged at all, I would have said something completely different.

"Aunty Margaret loved a drink, a fag, a good book and a bet on the races. She was very much like my Dad, often hilarious and had his kind, gentle nature, but could get fired up after a few stouts. Life and people were very cruel to her, but she strived to do her best to please everyone. I loved her for who she was and especially for what she did for me. She gave me up and allowed two incredible people to raise me. For that alone, she will always be loved, honoured and remembered as my dearly-loved aunt and a truly remarkable woman."

The loss of Aunty Margaret came too soon after losing Dad and I began to constantly fear losing Mum. The birth of our fourth child was a wonderful time, but I was struggling with my mental health and an insanely busy family life. In 1993, a year before Mum died, we moved house and soon after I had my first panic attack.

141

I didn't even know what a panic attack was. My whole body seized up and the pain in my chest was terrifying. I was sweating and my mind was racing with incoherent thoughts and an overwhelming feeling of fear and dread. Andrew took me to hospital, both of us thinking I had suffered a heart attack. After numerous tests the diagnosis came back.

"We can only conclude that you suffered a panic attack," the doctor explained. "Have you been under any stress of late?"

I almost laughed and was a little embarrassed my episode wasn't something which I considered serious back then. I certainly didn't believe it would happen again, but that first attack was just the forerunner of the many years ahead dealing with Anxiety Disorder and agoraphobia.

I did my best to slow down and turned back to writing and researching my family history. It was my way of coping with the growing frustration of having been denied information of my biological father.

On impulse I decided to ring Aunty Margaret's eldest daughter, Helen, hoping she might be able to tell me anything, something, a clue which might at least give me somewhere to look.

She greeted me politely and was confused over what I was asking about.

"I'm not sure why you would think I would know about your birth father, Storm. I've long forgotten you were adopted by Uncle Wally and Aunty Lil. I'm afraid I don't know much about it at all."

Maybe I should have let it go, but years of anger and frustration suddenly culminated in a desperate outburst.

"But you know Aunty Margaret is my birth mother?"

"What?"

"You did know, didn't you?"

"That's not true."

"Yeah, it is. I'm sorry, Helen, I thought you knew."

There was silence on the other end. I deflated, knowing I should have tested the waters.

"Helen, are you there?"

It was her angry husband who answered. "What the hell did you just say? What's wrong with Helen?"

I told him everything and heard him gasp. "I'm going to hang up now..."

"No, don't." It was Helen and she took the phone again. "No, Storm, I didn't know, but that's just typical of Mum. Frankly, I shouldn't be surprised after she had Susan, and you only had to see that house..."

I gritted my teeth, wanting to rebuke her judgemental opinion of her mother. Instead, I kept it polite, apologised and promised not to pursue anything else.

"This makes you my sister, not my cousin," Helen said. "I need to talk to my husband, but I'll ring you, Storm. We need to talk."

A few weeks later Helen arranged for us to get together with Susan. I don't even know if she knew Susan's origins, but I wasn't going to be the one to tell her. I was sick of feeling bad about myself for simply wanting the truth. I can barely describe how fucked up I felt over all this for a long time, but I kept it to myself, even from Andrew. My meeting with Helen didn't help.

At first it went well with lots of tears and talking. We even took photos together and talked about nurturing our relationship as sisters. I was feeling excited about it and then, once again, I said the wrong thing.

"How should we go about telling Philip? He's my half-brother and..."

"No," Helen said firmly. "We can't tell Philip. He won't think this is a good thing at all. All this will do is confirm an already low opinion he has about Mum. This would break him. He wouldn't want to know."

My soul was crushed and suddenly I didn't want to be there anymore. I didn't want to have to deal with any more rejection or grief or being made to feel of no value. My existence, my relationship to these people... blood might be thicker than water but only when it flows with love and acceptance. Otherwise, it's just clotted with bitterness and judgement.

I didn't hear from Helen again and I'm okay with that. To this day Philip still doesn't know about my relationship to him and that's okay too. My value and sense of family is not defined by whom I'm blood-related to. It's in the people who love, support and accept me.

Part Three

FINDING ANSWERS

CHAPTER TWENTY-ONE

THE SEARCH BEGINS

By 1995 I had constructed a family tree with over a thousand names, but always in the back of my mind was a family I was yet to learn of. By then I was beginning to have doubts of Robin's claim to be my biological father but I'd promised myself I would not pursue it while he was alive.

I loved him dearly, and his wife and five children. They were my half-brothers and sisters, and it was always an awesome time when my and Robin's big families came together. Kids everywhere, chaos and loads of fun. We went camping at Bateman's Bay one year and Andrew had all the kids catching salmon. There was nothing worth sabotaging those wonderful moments or discrediting Robin's belief. So I did nothing until he had passed away in 2015.

Two years later I finally gave myself permission to search and it began with applying for my adoption papers. We had been living in New Zealand since 2001 and everything had to be done by email. At the same time, I took a DNA test and sent it off to await the results. The DNA test came back first.

Having done exhaustive research into Mum and Robin's family tree, I knew their heritage was predominantly English and the unique Germanic/French of Alsace Lorraine. This is what I wanted to see as I got ready to see my results.

My daughters were with me as I nervously logged into the website and navigated to the page. My hopes were flatly doused as I stared at the 62% share of Irish, Welsh and Scottish. There was only 25% English in me along with 12% Finnish. The rest was a small mix of Ukrainian and Uzbekistan, which astounded me somewhat, considering one of my books had been set entirely in Ukraine.

The results gave me a long list of people with whom I shared DNA. There were no Scottish or Welsh but a massive list of Irish.

"I'm Irish," I gasped, staring at the screen.

My children were thrilled. There was something very cool about being Irish. I even rang my dearest friend Gladys, my Irish neighbour who had known me forever. She roared with laughter when I told her.

"I told you," she said. "I *fecking* told you how Irish you look? Do you remember, Storm?"

I did. She'd said it many times and even remarked how Irish-looking were my beautiful raven-haired daughters with their stunning blue eyes. I thought of one of my main characters of the books I had written, Mairead Kavanagh, with her Irish background and beautiful name. I'd even written a feature-length screenplay set in Ireland.

Yet, through all the excitement, other emotions were stirring inside of me. I waited until I was alone that night, sat down and cried bitterly.

"You fucking bastards, you all lied to me. I don't even know who I am any more. I'm fifty-fucking-five years old and know nothing about myself. I hate the lot of you."

Over the next few weeks, I sank into depression and kept going over the results. I was distracted from my essential tasks of trying to finish and publish my sixth book, while in the midst of dealing with some of Andrew's family issues. It was the first time I couldn't get excited over releasing a book.

To cope, I also worked on this memoir hoping it might help voice my thoughts and emotions. My life was one big depressing distraction from the things I loved doing. Meanwhile, my daughters were still intrigued and trying to piece together who my biological father might be.

We had a clue. One of my shared matches was a woman whose surname Donnelly was completely unfamiliar to me, yet she was my first cousin, twice removed.

Mikyla had undertaken study into the workings of DNA, how the x and y chromosomes were passed down from parent to child. She came to me and said she would like to contact this woman's son.

"Yeah sure," I told her, not really caring one way or another. I was too concerned with how I was going to break all of this to Robin's children. And then I let it all out. "They think I'm their sister and now I have to tell them I'm not. How do I do that? What if they stop thinking of me as their family? There is so much of this which is just so unfair. I had a right to know. I had a fucking right to know years ago. I shouldn't be dealing this bullshit at my age."

Five years into my fifties had given me several maladies to deal with, menopause and insomnia being just two of them. My mental health had improved after a diagnosis of sleep apnoea and the use of a machine to help me breathe at night. I felt all my recovery being slowly undone.

My daughters' immense support throughout this time can't be spoken of highly enough. They were dealing with their own issues of life and yet kept enthusiastically searching and trying to keep my spirits up. I owed it to them to help make sense out of our chaotic family.

It was time to stop feeling sorry for myself and get some answers. The one thing I could bring to this search was thirty years of doing genealogy. I started researching every DNA match I had, studying their family trees and looking for connections.

Meanwhile Mikyla was busy exchanging emails with Rick, the son of my elusive cousin. He was equally intrigued by our connection and had also looked into how DNA worked. The research they did together was nothing short of astounding, but to do it credit I've asked Mikyla to explain it:

Using triangulations of DNA matches, searching their family trees and looking for common ancestors, we were able to eliminate or identify potential ancestors. Rick had already created known groups of DNA matches that led back to certain ancestors. When we were unable to match up to them we could eliminate those branches. With the addition of a large chunk of X-DNA (which can only be passed from mother to child or father to daughter) meant we could eliminate any male – male (father to son) paths in Rick's tree.

As Mikyla and Rick tackled the DNA connections I added names to a new family tree. Shaz dug up all their secrets in records and old newspapers and, bit by bit, we began to see connections through the families I was related to. We soon had a satisfying list of direct ancestors and their family names; Dineen and Garnaut, Kelly and Cosgriff, Kestel and Oyston. Several of their ancestors were from the Munster province of Ireland, particularly Cork. We then had to follow their journeys to Australia.

One of the setbacks was the size of these families. Being Irish Catholics, some of these families had over twenty children and every one of them had to be researched.

We had the children of adultery to deal with, and those born out of wedlock or given to another family because of financial desperation. It seems the 'good old days' were made up of a hell of a lot of people who weren't so good and were just fallible human beings like the rest of us. Unfortunately they had stringent rules and morals to uphold and their mistakes had to be hidden away, rather than risk bringing shame to the family.

It should have been a simple search starting with Rick's mother, but we kept coming to dead ends. After months of searching, we discovered why. Again, I'll let Mikyla explain.

We were able to identify a particular ancestral name of Dineen, which both Rick and I had obviously descended from. We had DNA-matches to many of their descendants and thankfully a lot of them had family trees. We contacted the rest. We quickly realized that Rick did not have any ancestors from this family in his known family tree.

This gave us the breakthrough we'd been looking for on Rick's side. A lack of any DNA connections to his maternal grandmother had meant he had one group of DNA matches that did not fit in with his known family tree and he had no relatives of their names. Rick had suspected his grandmother's parents were not her parents and now we had more proof of this. Rick's grandmother could have only been adopted from the Dineen family line.

The next interesting step was discovering that Rick and I both DNA-matched to a certain Dineen gentleman. I also had DNA connections to his wife while Rick shared no DNA with her or her descendants. This meant that our connection was through the one great-grandparent. I was then able to use the DNA matches leading back to his wife to work out the next step in our lineage. Rick was left with a great-grandfather but no great-grandmother as yet.

After a year, we had constructed and researched a family tree of over three thousand people. We learned of their heartbreaks, their losses, their triumphs and family events. We searched for them in newspapers and read their letters, their wills, their obituaries and their tombstones, and we did it reverently. They were more than just names. They were real people with real lives.

CHAPTER TWENTY-TWO

MY ADOPTION PAPERS

In October 2018, my adoption papers arrived through my email. I'd like to say I was excited and nervous, but instead I was becoming weary of searching and getting nowhere. It was as if all this had become a cruel game. Every new clue just led to a dead end and I was beginning to think I'd be better off giving up.

Loyal readers of my fiction books were patiently waiting for me to finish the fourth and final book of a series. I hated letting them down, but I couldn't concentrate on writing it well and I wasn't about to ruin the series with a half-hearted plot. I had to accept that particular book would have to wait.

To compensate my neglect, I wrote something much easier, an erotic Western which was just fun and fantasy, and took me only six weeks to write. I still had to edit and format if for publication; as well as design a cover and promote it. Knowing my time was limited, I decided to send it off to a publisher in the United States, rather than publish it myself. I didn't expect to hear from them for a while, but three days later I got an email back. They wanted my book.

It was a huge relief and allowed me to get back to my obsessive searching and let them do all the work. It gave me a chance to breathe while also dealing with ongoing health problems and other family issues, including the loss of Andrew's parents.

I desperately needed those adoption papers to tell me something so I didn't have to do this any longer. I was over it, exhausted, but still unable to detach myself because I had to know. At 56 years old, I couldn't comprehend or deal with the thought of not knowing.

This is something adoptees know well. During this time, I spoke with two of my sisters-in-law, both of them adoptees. We shared our experiences, frustrations and desperation, and it astounded me how they both knew exactly what I was feeling. They had made good progress in their own searches and I was happy for them, but envious. Why did my history have to be so complicated? Why had Aunty Margaret been so stubborn? She could have told me all of it and saved me from this grief.

I had gone through every worst case scenario. Was she raped, and how I would feel knowing I was a product of something so vile? I honestly don't know, but I figured I wouldn't be the first child born of violence. .

I wanted to scream out to her, "You had nothing to be ashamed of. None of this was your fault. I wouldn't have blamed you for anything. I have nothing but love and respect for you. I just wish you could have trusted me enough to tell me."

I opened my adoption papers with no expectations. The words on the very first page were sobering. On the 24th November 1961, their application to adopt Susan was marked 'deleted', exactly ten months after her birth. It was good knowing that a few months earlier Michael had come into my parents' lives, and saved them from the despair of losing another child.

Immediately under it was a date of 16th February 1963, six weeks after my birth. This page was followed by the application which had been submitted in November of that year. I was immediately curious as to why it had taken so long to set the process in motion. The application read:

"In the matter of the Adoption of Children Act of 1943, and in the matter of an application by Walter Taylor and Lilian Taylor of Eastwood, to adopt Storm Catherine Peters, a female illegitimate child born in January. The application will be heard at the Police Court, Adelaide on Wednesday 29th January 1964."

As it was, there was little information about my biological father other than his name, Steven Williams, which Aunty Margaret had already told me. The papers gave his approximate age of 32 and that he was living in Penola, South Australia in 1962, at the time of my conception.

But other information in my adoption papers provided me with something unexpected; a portal back in time, a glimpse of my first year and a snapshot of my parents. I could almost hear their voices.

Due to the privacy of others, I can only summarise the next page, because it was Aunty Margaret's affidavit attesting to her desire to allow Mum and Dad to adopt me. It had detailed information of her circumstances, supporting what Mum and Dad had told me about her unhappy marriage and the financial poverty she was abandoned to.

With her statement was that certain description of me stated again.

I became associated with a man and as a result of that association, I gave birth to an illegitimate female child.

It felt as if she was confessing to a crime. I sensed her shame and my heart ached for her.

The following pages were reports by the social worker in charge of monitoring my welfare in the lead up to my adoption.

12ᵗʰ February 1963

I called on Mrs Peters regarding another illegitimate child and she told me of the birth of this other baby and stated she had given the baby for adoption to her brother. I called in at his home address at 1.30 pm, but found no one there.

14ᵗʰ February 1963

Storm Catherine Peters:
Small baby, 6lbs at birth but looks well, nicely dressed and well cared for. Bassinet is in the foster parents' bedroom. House is clean and tidy as is the appearance of the foster mother.

Called again at this home and interviewed Mr and Mrs Taylor. They admitted to the arrangement and they are prepared to adopt this child and lodge an application. These people occupy an older type stone attached place with an iron roof which is not in good repair on the outside. There are five rooms of lounge, kitchen-dinette, two bedrooms and one which is used as a storeroom but which can be made into a bedroom for the baby.

Mrs Taylor was most difficult to interview. She was unwilling to talk, reluctant to give any details and everything I got had to be prised out of her. Also in the home I saw a four-year old Aborigine child. She later admitted she had been fostering this child for over a year.

151

I saw both the serious and the funny sides of her interaction with Mum and having to 'prise' information out of her. This was classic Mum who didn't like people knowing her business, but I also sensed the fear she must have felt with this woman's unannounced arrival. They had two children, neither who legally belonged to them.

It was ignorant and completely unnecessary to presume Michael to be indigenous, based solely on his dark skin, especially when in a later report, he is referred to as Indian. Four-year old boy would have sufficed and ethnicity left out of it.

7th March 1963

Mr and Mrs Taylor called by appointment to discuss their application. The illegitimate child of Mr Taylor's sister has been in their care since birth. They collected her from the hospital.

Mrs Taylor is still a hard, sour woman, but as she is a staunch member of the Salvation Army, queried our information that this couple drink to excess. Mrs Taylor vehemently denied this and pointed out that Mr Taylor in his job, one of his duties is to stop other barmen from drinking, therefore he could not and must not do so.

The foster child who looks Indian, was placed with Mrs Taylor by the Captain of the Salvation Army group which she attends. This child is visited weekly by his mother and the child told me he had two mummies.

There was much discussion over telling the baby girl about her adoption. Their attitude to this and the child's future is in general very vague and only fair after some discussion seemed to improve.

I remonstrated Mrs Taylor over the name Storm which she has chosen for the child and advised that some magistrates would not be prepared to grant an adoption order with a word and not a real name. They will discuss this further. Mr Taylor will ask his sister to contact the Department regarding consent etc.

I really didn't like this woman, especially with her remonstrating Mum over my name and, in her limited opinion, not a real name, just a word. And again with Michael's ethnicity. She would have been surprised to learn Michael's biological father was from Cyprus in Greece and a mother of English heritage.

From the cold, rigid formality of this social worker's report, something else was emerging for me; a portal back in time allowing me to see events playing out.

I laughed reading Mum's vehement denial of hers and Dad's excess drinking, and laughed even more at why such an accusation was impossible. Really Mum? Because of Dad setting the example and keeping his barmen from drinking? This was the man who challenged one of his mates to beat his twelve-year old daughter in downing a pint of beer. Of course I did Dad proud and won the bet for him, but Dad was never going to set an example for any of them.

There was a lack of Dad's input throughout the reports. Mum did all the talking. This was how it always was; Dad saying little and Mum taking charge, such was his confidence in her.

The next report came in August when I was seven months old and it resonated with trouble brewing behind the scenes.

Nice baby, well cared for, looked well and suitably dressed. Bassinet in parents' room. House is clean and tidy as is the appearance of the foster mother.

I saw both Mr and Mrs Taylor. Mrs Taylor was her usual off-hand self. When asked if the sister-in-law Mrs Peters had been to the Department to sign the consent, she said, "Ask him, he's dealing with it."

Mr Taylor admitted that his sister is very difficult and has become more so recently. She frequently visits the house and will not be definite. As he is due for holidays, he will bring his sister into the Department. Mrs Taylor stated that she is happy to keep the baby as things are but would like to make it 'legal.'

Mrs Taylor cannot understand why the name Storm is objected to and claims 'there are plenty of girls called Gail, so what's the difference?' (Great point, Mum). She says that this child will live in a modern age and the teenagers she knows think it's fabulous.

Mum's defiance was obvious, but the sadder part of this report was the mention of Aunty Margaret 'being difficult.' She was questioning her decision to give me up, and from what I experienced in my childhood, it was years before she was at peace with it.

The next report came two months later and, again, Mum had me laughing. It seemed Dad may have gently pointed out how her abrupt attitude might hinder the process. She wasn't doing them any favours by being rude to this social worker, so Mum took a different approach. She was a very adaptable woman.

24th October 1963

Baby is clean, looks well and suitably dressed. Cot is in the parents' bedroom. The house is clean and tidy and the foster mother is neat and clean.

Storm has grown into a beautiful baby. She is a very attractive child and a very active one. Mrs Taylor is unconcerned about not having the consent for the adoption of this child but will ask her husband to do something about it again. She knows that Margaret is working full time.

The change in Mrs Taylor's manner on this occasion is amazing. I was greeted like a long lost friend, invited in and taken to the kitchen where they were having lunch. Mrs Taylor offered me a cup of tea, chatted freely and walked me to the gate.

On the 22nd November 1963, Aunty Margaret finally gave her consent for Mum and Dad to adopt me. At the end of January 1964, they had their day in court. The judge also made comments about their wisdom in naming me Storm, but in the end declared them to be my legal parents. I couldn't be happier about that decision.

Mum and Dad could never afford a camera and there are no baby pictures of me before the age of one. Even then, I only have a few pictures of myself as a child. What my adoption papers provided was even better, capturing my first year with Mum and Dad and the memories I have of them.

Oh, Mum, you're were such a character and I could just picture this poor woman's dealings with you; and Dad, as always, you were quietly there quietly guiding, yet having full confidence in Mum to sort things out. Thank you both for fighting for me and for my wonderful name, and thank you too, Aunty Margaret, for loving me enough to give me up.

CHAPTER TWENTY-THREE

2019

Two years and a lot of money had gone into searching for my biological father through DNA. As the New Year commenced, Mikyla finally got a breakthrough. As I still struggle understanding the technicalities, I've asked Mikyla to explain what happened.

A second DNA test with another company had brought stronger and better results leading to more DNA-matched relatives. I straight away started going through the trees of the new matches and quickly came up against that name from past research, Dineen. I started sending emails to several of these people, especially those who didn't have family trees I could check.

The first reply came back with a, "Yes, I am a descendant of that family."

I can't describe what I felt at that moment, shocked, stunned, thrilled... With this final evidence, I sent my theory to Rick for confirmation and sure enough, Rick found the same family line in his DNA matches. He also contacted the family and soon we had numerous people who were all descended from the same line and related to both myself and Rick.

The final confirmation came from the Dineen ancestor from whom Rick and Mum were both descended. His daughter had married into the Garnaut family which was Mum's family line. We now had a complete family tree leading down to Mum's biological grandparents.

I messaged my sister, Shaz, to find anything she could about these people and she quickly came back with an extensive research and a family website with a detailed biography and photographs. The family resemblance was indisputable. It was time to share all of this with Mum.

Over a morning coffee with my girls, Mikyla shared the news.

"Mum, we worked it out. Rick and I have discussed it, done all the calculations. We know which family it is. We know who your grandmother is and one of her sons is your father."

I was stunned and not immediately able to accept what she was telling me, but a simple Google search ended my doubts. We found a photo of one of the sons, one of my biological uncles, and my whole world went spinning around me.

"I look like him. I look just like him."

The resemblance was uncanny, but Mikyla was quick to point out extenuating circumstances were yet to be factored in.

"It's possible this woman had a son and adopted him out before her marriage, and we're yet to fully confirm all of the DNA connections, but we're confident, Mum. These people are your family, your grandparents and your very closely-related family."

The possibility of another son born before her marriage needed to be considered, especially since none of them were named Steven Williams. Perhaps a son who had been adopted by a Williams family. I also had to consider the probability of Aunty Margaret inventing that name. It still haunts me knowing she had such a bizarre determination to keep her secret. I can only hope no other secrets are lurking.

Mikyla's pronouncement was a surreal moment, an accomplishment of countless hours and months of frustrations and dead ends. Between them Mikyla and Rick had exchanged over 300 emails to get to this point.

Yes, I was still to pinpoint the one who was my biological father, but suddenly it didn't matter anymore. I could see his family and was even able to read quite a bit about them through internet searches. We laughed to see so many of them were writers.

It was a little sad they would never get to know me, but I have no wish to contact them and risk rejection or cause any unwelcome surprises. I had been down that road with Aunty Margaret's children and wasn't about to do it again.

It's enough to have come this far and, more importantly, understand that family has little to do with blood or DNA. It's about those people who are always around somewhere, whether near or far or just in a photo on the shelf. It's those people who have shared in your happiness, supported you

156

through hard times, celebrated in good times and simply accepted you as theirs, as the person you are.

We continue to add to this family tree and learn more about them while we rule out all other possibilities. Have I got a definite answer? No, but we have strong suspicions. What I have is a deeply satisfying answer which gives me closure, peace and an insight into my heritage. Maybe I'll have more to write in time to come.

Earlier this year Rick and his partner, Trish, came to Invercargill to visit us. It was a wonderful moment meeting and being with these people who are my family, connected to a father I never knew. We caught up again in Adelaide where I met Rick's daughter and they met with my youngest son. Rick also met another cousin from our new family line and has established a close friendship.

It has been wonderful to see my daughters getting so passionately involved in our family history. As much as it is my legacy, it is theirs and my sons' as well. It's something to look back upon and see the people our family are made up of; to see the women who fought against incredible odds.

This is where my story should have ended, but Mikyla wasn't quite finished searching.

"Mum, have you ever followed up on that 'missing person' report for your brother?"

I laughed. "It's been 34 years, love. We would have heard something long before now. I'm sad to say Michael's dead and buried somewhere."

She persisted. "Would you mind if I followed it up?"

"Go for it," I said. "But be prepared to be disappointed. I'm afraid that's one mystery in my life which I'll never have an answer to."

Within weeks I was about to find out how very wrong I could be.

* * * * *

On the 3rd February 2019 I brought up a picture of Michael on my computer.

"Happy 60th birthday, Michael. Whatever happened to you, you old bugger? Anyway, wherever you are, I love you and hope you know I'm always thinking of you."

A couple of weeks later the phone rang. I recognised Julie's voice immediately and gulped with guilt.

"Julie, a very Happy Birthday for yesterday and yes, I did remember it was your birthday and I was going to post on Facebook and then I got side-tracked and I know I'm bloody useless and..."

"Storm, would you shut up, just shut up and listen."

I could hear the urgency in her voice and was immediately concerned. "Is everything alright Jules?"

"Um... no... um. I got a phone call yesterday."

"Are the boys alright Jules?"

"Yeah, yes. It's not about the boys. Everyone's okay, but you should sit down. I've got something to tell you."

I did sit down. "I'm listening."

"I got a phone call yesterday, from Darren, an officer in 'Missing Persons' here in Adelaide. I don't know how to tell you this..."

I knew what it was about, remembering Mikyla's request to contact 'missing persons' and follow up the report we'd lodged thirty years ago.

"Oh god, Jules, you're not going to be telling me... Oh fuck, what the fuck has happened?"

I heard the crack of emotion in her voice. "He was alive, Storm. All these years, Mick was fucking alive."

I could barely breathe. "Is he... is he still...?"

"No, Storm, no, he's not. I'm sorry. Oh fuck, this is hard. There's so much. I can barely get my head around it."

"Just tell me, Jules."

"Alright, but this isn't going to be easy. Mick was alive and, as far as Darren knows, until 2009 and um... oh Storm, he was living in New Zealand."

"Are you fucking kidding me?" My mind was spinning. "Where? Where in New Zealand?"

Jules attempted to say the name and I finished it for her. "Whakatane."

I tried to get up and had to sit down again. "Keep going."

"I haven't got much. All this guy knows at the moment is that he was there at some point and he died in Wellington..."

"What? Wellington?"

The moment she said it, a memory erupted in my mind and played out as if it was on a screen in front of me. I shook my head, uncertain if my brain in the state-of-shock was playing tricks with my mind.

"Are you alright, Storm?"

"Yeah, just tell me all of it."

"Like I said, there's not much, but Storm, he... Storm, he had another kid. Darren says her name is Fredom."

I laughed and immediately burst into tears. "What a beautiful name and so fucking typical of Michael. Oh, god, I'm so sorry Jules... I'm not even thinking. This must be killing you."

"I'm not good, no, but yeah... typical fucking Mick. It is a beautiful name."

"And so significant," I smiled. "That's all he ever wanted. Freedom. He was such a fucking hippy with shit like that."

Julie laughed. "Remember what he wanted to call Clinton? Sunshine... fucking Sunshine, but I drew the line."

We had a laugh together, allowing me to recoup some strength.

"Jules, how... how did he die?"

"I don't know, honey. Darren is trying to get more details and..."

"How the fuck are we hearing this now? Thirty-four fucking years later... How the hell do we not know this?"

"Tell me about it. I'm fucking wild and..."

"Oh, my god... the boys... Clinton, does he know?"

"Not yet. How do I tell him? How do I tell him the father he fucking loved was still alive all that time, and had another kid? This will kill him."

Suddenly, I didn't want it to be about my grief or whatever I was feeling. There were two boys, not boys, men, my brother's sons, the nephews I love. Their whole world was about to be shattered and yet...

"Oh, hell, Jules, I didn't think... When Mikyla asked about the 'Missing Person' report... Oh, god, Jules, what have I done?"

"You opened up a huge fucking can of worms," she laughed softly, trying to reassure me she wasn't angry. "It's alright, Storm. We'll deal with it."

"I'm so sorry, Jules... I know I should be fucking angry at Michael right now... for what he's done... to your boys, to you, but... he was my brother and

I love him, I fucking love him, and he was alive, living in the same country as me all that time and..."

I collapsed in tears; my whole body was shaking with utter despair. Every childhood memory; every visit to prisons and boys' homes, every special moment we'd shared, Michael and me, was flashing through my head.

I could hear Julie. "Aw Storm, I'm so sorry, honey."

"No," I wept. "I'm sorry. I'm so fucking sorry about everything. You're the one who suffered, you and the boys..."

"And you loved him. You stuck by him. I know you're hurting too."

"I need answers. Let's get some answers."

I pulled myself together and went over to my laptop. "I'm bringing up Facebook. I'm going to find his daughter. What surname do you reckon she would have? Never mind, I'll try them all... Taylor, Mairou, Robinson... what other aliases did he use? There were plenty of them."

While I was talking and typing, the name came up almost immediately. "Oh fuck, Jules. I've found her."

On the screen was a beautiful girl, dark skin, dark eyes, black hair... There were pictures of her children.

"Oh wow," I smiled. "One of her kids... I can see your boys. They're all lovely, just beautiful."

"Are there any of Mick?"

I started going through all her pictures and suddenly froze as a name came up. I stared, trying to choke back tears, trembling and feeling I was about to pass out.

"Are you alright, Storm?"

I couldn't breathe and could just barely get out. "Hang on. I'll ring back."

I got up and wandered aimlessly about the room and then into the lounge room where my grief spilled over.

For thirty-four years it had been easier to believe he was dead. To dare to imagine him being alive somewhere meant raising questions about what we had meant to each other; questions I hadn't dared to ask out loud for fear I would never know and, if I did, would I get the answers I wanted?

Did you ever think of me, Michael? Did you ever remember the fun we had as kids, the nights we slept at the front door; those times we got up in the middle of the night to cook pancakes? Did you ever remember I was there

160

for you? Or did you just forget me? Did I never matter to you as much as you mattered to me?

Somehow, I think Michael had known what I would ask. He knew I would always be thinking of him and he'd had an answer waiting for me for many years, waiting for me to find it, even beyond the grave.

When I was able to, I rang Julie back. "Sorry, Jules, I just needed a moment. Michael had three children, not one. He named them..."

I had to breathe again, because it was impossible to say their names without the threat of falling apart.

"What is it, honey?"

"Aw, Jules. I loved him... I fucking loved him."

"I know you did, hun."

"You and the boys deserved just so much more than this. My heart's breaking for you, and I should be furious with him for what's he done... but I can't. I'm so sorry Jules, and now he's fucked me up again. Thirty-four years later, that bastard is still able to reduce me to this."

"What happened?"

"He has a son and called him Thunda." I smiled. "He got it wrong, typical Michael, but I know what he was thinking. If I'd been a boy, Dad was going to call me Thor after the god of thunder. Michael thought that name was awesome, and he remembered all those years, but he must have forgotten the Thor part or just decided he preferred Thunda."

"Oh wow, that's awesome, hun."

"Yeah, but there's more." I felt my throat constricting again with emotion. "He had another girl, his eldest girl. She's beautiful too and you know what he called her?"

I think Julie knew but she let me say it.

"That bloody bastard of a brother of mine... He was thinking of me, Jules. He really did care about me and he let me know it. He called her Storm. That beautiful girl, Michael's daughter, she has my name."

I thought of Mum and Dad's fight to give me that name. In childhood, I'd been teased about it and throughout my life I had been questioned about its origins. None of us expected my name to become something so significant. It was now more than just my awesome first name. It was the answer to my questions and Michael's final message to me, telling me I was remembered and loved.

EPILOGUE

In the weeks and months after Julie's phone call, too much has happened to relate it all in one chapter. I've decided another book may follow but, for now, I need this one to be finished and be read by the many people who need to hear this story.

I have been told Michael passed away in Wellington in 2009. Thunda sent me records which were by no means easy to read. They were heart-breaking. Michael died of liver cancer which also caused dementia and need for intervention by social services. It only confirmed the memory which erupted so abruptly during my phone call with Julie.

In 2007 I was in Wellington, catching up with a dear friend. One early evening we returned to the city, and I went into the 24/7 to buy my cigarettes. When I came out I noticed a man sitting on the pavement across the road. He was leaning against a building and staring out at nothing in particular. His hair was long, black and heavily streaked with grey, as was his facial hair.

After six years of working with the homeless, it was my habit to make sure they were alright whenever I saw them, especially if they were asleep. Being told to 'fuck off' was far better than me wondering if they were sleeping or sick. This man didn't raise any alarms for me or look in need of assistance, but my gaze lingered for a moment.

"He looks a bit like my brother," I whispered to myself, smiling sadly at how absurd that was.

Now I'm not so sure. Did I dream it, or did the shock of finding out about Michael revive a real memory. I keep thinking about it and it's devastating believing I may have come that close to Michael.

Recently I have connected with Michael's New Zealand family but am yet to meet them, something I plan to rectify early next year.

In 2015 Michael's children had attempted a search for his Adelaide family, but instead someone tracked down his birth parents. Michael's biological father was deceased but had four children, the eldest of whom he named Michael. I've recently connected with him and hope to get to know this family as well.

Michael's son, Thunda, was the first one I spoke to over the phone. He was wonderful and made me feel at ease with his kind words. He told me of how these families had all got together and made a Facebook page for Michael.

I received an invitation to join and I accepted. Going through the posts, I was stunned to see my brother's birth mother Mary and half-sister Kelly were also a part of it. At first I was distressed seeing all these people who had their own connections to Michael. I'd had no good thoughts of his birth parents, having formed a very negative opinion over a life time. It was Julie and her boys I was concerned for, knowing how brutal this revelation had been for them.

As with every hurdle in my life, I wrote and prayed about it and finally acknowledged God has already given me everything I needed to deal with this: forgiveness, and a constant reminder to walk a mile in someone's shoes before ever making assumptions.

With some reservations I finally made my first post, introducing myself and posting some pictures of Michael. I was overwhelmed by the warm welcome I received from everyone. I knew then how much I wanted to meet these people.

In April, Andrew and I made a trip to Adelaide to see our children. Our eldest son and his partner had just become the proud parents of our beautiful twin grandchildren. Our youngest son had moved back to Adelaide a year earlier and was loving being an uncle.

We cherished our time with them all and reflected on how far we had come. It was also a time to be with Julie and Michael's eldest son, hopeful of soothing their wounds. My brother had abandoned them and I wasn't about to justify it. All I could do was find answers, and one of them was already being worked upon.

Soon after joining the Facebook page, I was contacted by Michael's birth mother, Mary. She wanted to talk to me about her part in Michael's life. Knowing I would soon be in Adelaide, we arranged a time to get together, though I was very cynical about it.

We go by what we know and run with it. For fifty-odd years I had been aware of a woman's name which had just always seemed imbedded in our family history, so much so, I had even researched and added her family tree to mine.

During those years I had formed an opinion of her, based on her absence from Michael's life. And so it was with a rather cynical outlook I prepared myself to meet her at the Beehive Corner on Easter Monday. On the drive to the city, I sat in the Uber reminding myself to be polite, to keep emotion out of it and be prepared to listen, but a real negativity simmered inside me.

It was a lovely day in Adelaide, and once the meeting was over I planned to meet my sons at the cinema in Hindley Street. Seeing a good movie with my boys would be the perfect pick-me-up in case my spirits were low.

Right on time, I saw three women approaching and my anxiety went up a notch. It was beyond surreal as a woman I had known of all my life, but had never seen, was suddenly embracing me. I was then introduced to her daughter Kelly and granddaughter Alana. We all nervously greeted each other and made a quick decision to go for coffee at the Pancake Kitchen.

As we ordered I took in the sight of this woman, knowing she was nearly eighty and barely looked a day over sixty. She was petite and smartly dressed, reminding me a lot of Mum.

We sat down and Mary removed her sunglasses, causing me to gasp a little.

"What is it?" she asked, noticing my very involuntary reaction.

Tears were pricking at my eyes. "It's just that... well, it's just that I'm kind of looking back at the eyes of my nephew. I always wondered where he'd got his eyes from."

I saw an instant shine of emotion in her blue/green eyes and suddenly understood how wrong I had been. This was someone who had suffered just as much and for far longer than I had, whatever the circumstances. In that moment, I let go of my bitterness and allowed myself to experience the real connection between us, the shared despair of having lost someone we both loved.

For the next two and a half hours we talked and listened and cried a lot. I was humbled by this woman who had known many hard times, more than I had ever experienced. I felt ashamed for having held anything against her and considered including her story in this book. But it wasn't mine to tell, and I have since decided we need to be together to do it, for me to get it down in her words. We have plans underway.

It was wonderful to hear her remembering Mum and Dad with fondness, and thereby affirming many things I had remembered and been told.

"Your Mum wanted Michael so much. She begged me to let her adopt him and she kept asking me to promise her, that I wouldn't ever take him away from her."

I could almost hear the echoes of the past and sorely wished Michael had known how much he was loved by his two Mums; two women who had experienced so much suffering, hardship and heartbreak.

When it was time for me to leave I wanted to stay, reluctant to let go of her, wanting to know more and afraid of not seeing her again. I promised to try to catch up again before we returned to New Zealand, but our time was gone before we knew it.

The women walked with me to the cinemas and I introduced them to my sons before our final goodbyes. A good movie and even better company was the perfect balm on my worn-out emotions.

Later that night I spoke with Julie. "You'll love her. I promise. She's lovely and so is her daughter and granddaughter."

A few nights after that, I was able to share the news with my nephew Clinton and show him the pictures I had taken that day.

"I'm so sorry, Clinton. I can't imagine what you're going through. I'm sorry my brother was such a shit father to do what he did to you, but I'd really like you to know something. You have a grandmother, a really lovely grandmother, who would welcome you with so much love anytime you wanted. I know Mum and Dad were your Nanna and Pa, but I know they would want this for you too."

Julie has since met up with Mary and as predicted, loved her. Clinton is yet to decide how much he's prepared to allow into his life.

While in Adelaide, Julie and I caught up with Darren, the officer from 'Missing Persons' who had initially received Mikyla's email. I was truly moved by his concern and remorse for us, dealing with a system that failed us. We should have been told. Julie and I had filed the original report and we were the last to know of Michael's fate. Darren had experienced many sleepless nights as his investigations continued to meet dead ends.

He and another officer took us for coffee where we talked. At one stage he grinned at me.

"You actually found more out about Michael's movements in New Zealand than we or the New Zealand police had found."

I laughed. "I do genealogy. We make great detectives."

We got to talking about what had started all this - the search for my birth father.

"By the way," I smiled, peering at Darren. "One of my biological father's family is a copper, rather high up in the ranks and been around a long time. It's someone you might know."

"Go on," Darren said. "Are you going to tell me who?"

I did and watched Darren's jaw drop. "Do I look like him?"

Darren slowly nodded, completely aghast.

"You might want to keep that one to yourself," I laughed. "I have no plans of contacting any of them. I'm at peace with it now. A lot of wounds have been opened through all this and I have no desire for me or anyone else to be hurt. I want to mourn my brother, unite a family and put the past to rest."

But what a small world; and if we truly want peace, we can only navigate it with compassion and acceptance. We need to forgive if we want to end our days without regrets. There are too many broken lives. Best just to get on with it and know everyone is hurting, one way or another.

I'm still in shock over how our quest to find a biological father became such an epic family journey. There were as many casualties along the way as there were triumphant moments. The emotional toll was enormous, and not mine alone.

Mikyla took on the burden of having stirred up a bitter past for Julie and Clinton.

"I should never have sent that email. Perhaps we were all better off not knowing."

I disagreed. "This is not your fault, love. I wanted to know, no matter how painful the truth was. This began long before you sent an email. It began years before I was even born. Some people chose to keep secrets and those secrets caused a lot of pain for generations to come, but it stops here. Our family will never have secrets, because we know how to talk to one another, we have compassion and we don't judge anyone. There's nothing you children can't come to us with, and you know Dad and I will only have love and support waiting for you, just as my parents had for Michael and me."

There's still so much more I could write, my life after 1985; my years in social work, film and theatre and my writing career, but for now this part of my life story ends.

Next year, I'll take it up again and probably write another book. For now, this author goes back to writing erotic fiction where I get to dictate the rules for my characters, though often they have minds of their own and I'm just required to keep up with them.

For me, 56 years of mysteries are finally resolved. I'm at peace and looking forward to the future. This year, Andrew and I will be celebrating 35 years married. We've been blessed with four amazing children and six beautiful grandchildren. My life has been full and happy, and I have no regrets.

And with a bit of a growl and a grin, I have to acknowledge Michael's remarkable achievements as well, but not so much his way of achieving them. Five children and eleven grandchildren that I know of at this stage.

There are still questions to be answered and I hope to have all the answers in the coming year. For now, this is us signing off,

Illegitimately yours,
Michael and me

ACKNOWLEDGEMENTS

Writing my first non-fiction book was one of the most challenging projects of my writing career. None of it would have been possible without so many people helping me and getting on board with the research and book production.

First up, I need to thank my daughters Mikyla and Shaz who have been with me throughout this entire process, doing the months of research and supporting me through some emotional times. Mikyla's relentless search to find my biological family was incredible; having to learn about the workings of DNA and apply it to the lineages of the families. Shaz was on the case of finding individuals and digging into their backgrounds to bring out all the secrets.

My gratitude and thanks must go to my cousin Rick whose tireless efforts helped us to solve the DNA connections, with Rick and Mikyla exchanging hundreds of emails and tackling each new hurdle of DNA and genealogical research.

Reading a good story is always so much easier when it is edited professionally. Once again, my wonderful husband Andrew was right beside me, finding those endless typos and advising me on sentence structure, allowing me to produce a good second draft. His feedback and encouragement have kept me breathing.

The draft was then sent off to be polished by Edna, an editing extraordinaire. My first time working with Edna was simply amazing and her command of words, commas and grammar are second to none. My deepest thanks and sincere gratitude for lending me her extraordinary talent.

It was also my privilege and delight to once again team up with Leah, the brilliant photographer and artist who was with my on most of my book covers, beginning with The Finest Line in 2012. With Leah was my daughter Shaz who came up with the idea for the cover. Together, they are creative genius and their work is deeply appreciated.

With this story touching on so many lives, it was vital to establish facts from various friends and family. My heartfelt thanks goes to Julie, Clinton and Jamin who have a hefty emotional investment in this story.

To Lee and Kelly, such wonderful women who gave me the purpose of this book, to be one of empathy, healing, forgiveness and love.

To Storm, Thunda and Fredom, who have welcomed me and given me the joy of knowing my brother's life after he disappeared from mine. In them, I see Michael and his memory is kept alive in their beautiful faces and warm hearts.

To Diane, my best friend since our schooldays, who introduced me to my soul mate: remembering and writing about our days growing up together has been a privilege and an honour. Thank you for being there for me through some difficult years.

Once again, my sincere thanks goes to the members of our writing group Southern Scribes. You read, advised and encouraged me throughout the two years of working on this project, and you kept me on track to get it finished. Your advice and friendship is cherished.

As I've mentioned, this was a difficult book to write and only possible with the support of my beautiful family to whom this book is dedicated with love.

Made in the USA
Monee, IL
17 July 2020